Alpine Elephant
In Hannibal's Tracks

by
JOHN HOYTE

WIPF & STOCK · Eugene, Oregon

1

Contents

Plates

(Between Pages 132 – 139)

With acknowledgements to those whose names

are shown in brackets

Maps

Acknowledgements

The expedition would like to express its most sincere thanks to the following, who generously helped it.

Equipment Lotus Ltd.-and in particular Mr. Tysoe of the Northampton factory for the four elephant boots.

The Flaxspinners Association of Great Britain and John Smith (Blanket Makers) for the combined manufacture of the elephant jacket.

William Kingham & Sons Ltd., for provisions.

Kunzle Ltd., for a special elephant cake and other provisions. Newbold & Bulford Ltd., for pedometer and compass.

Institut Geographique National of France for large scale maps. Haythornwaite & Sons Ltd., for Grenfell jackets.

Advice or information: on the academic side

Dr. A.H. McDonald. Sir Gavin de Beer.

Dr. M.A. de Lavis-Trafford. Professor Amedeo Mainri of Naples.

Abdel Aziz Driss, curator of the museum of Bardo, Tunisia (near Carthage).

C. Blair Esq., Victoria and Albert Museum. Professor Vittorio Morone of Turin.

Dr. Julian de Zulueta-of the World Health Organisation. Senator Sibille.

General Guillaume. Major Alexant.

Assistance in the planning and completion of the actual journey

The British Consuls at Turin, Lyon and Geneva. Signor Maraldi of the Italian Embassy, London.

Acknowledgements

Mr. John Greenwood and Dr. Guerrieri of the Italian State Tourist Dept., London.

Hammond & Co. Ltd., Insurance Brokers.

Monsieur Pinget, Chief of the Maurienne frontier police.

The French and Italian Customs Officials.

Angelo Airaghi, Giuseppe Sicari and all the others in the University Reception committee at Rome.

The Press

The staff of the News Chronicle and especially M r. Ian Colquhoun, Chief Assistant Editor, Stephen Barker and John Silverside.

The staff of Life magazine and especially, Dick Pollard, London

Life Editor, Timothy Green, David Lees and Pierre Boulat.

Alexandre—for international television filming.

From Turin

Dr. John May for interpreting and preparing extremely suitable lecture programmes for the expedition lecture at Rome.

Signor Terni-for providing the elephant and all kinds of other things and who cannot be thanked enough for all he has done.

Jumbo-for full co-operation and comradeship, and, we hope, for not adding to the mumbo !

There are many others we should like to thank, foremost amongst these being the mayors of all the towns at which we stopped along the route and all the local people whose enthusiasm, spontaneity and generosity were overwhelming.

I am also grateful to Dr. A. H. McDonald for checking through the classical sections of the script.

PART ONE

BUILD-UP

CHAPTER I

Prologue

It is a lovely morning. The wind comes helter-skelter down the long hillside and playfully tosses the branches of the mountain ash into wild patterns of movement. Overhead, the billowing clouds race across the sky and as they catch the brilliant, early morning sunshine they radiate delicate shades of translucent colour. Beyond stands the great, serene, azure dome of heaven, fading to a soft green near the horizon, in vivid contrast to the dynamic colouring and motion of the clouds. As far as the eye can see, mountains raise their mighty heads in wide, generous sweeps and then plunge through dark pinewoods to the deep valleys. Great purple shadows and glowing patches of sunlight chase each other across their brows, climb to the top-most crags in furious haste and then vanish beyond into some hidden secret valley in the wind blown race. It is on such a day that one feels at one's best. Earth and sky, light and shade, wind and sudden stillness, the momentary scent of the pinewoods and brilliant colours spread out in lavish beauty, all conspire to create a profound harmony between the watcher and the moving spirit behind Nature.

Here is a road; a high, winding track, lonely and lost. It seems to come from nowhere and to lead to nowhere. Two figures appear and stand starkly silhouetted against the bright horizon. They have just come around a bend in the path and stop to survey the panorama, which now suddenly stretches itself before them, to a skyline of mountain peak and eternal snow. They might be any two friends, but we conclude that they are not locals. One looks as if he might be of Eastern origin and the other, possibly English. Their voices are carried over in the fitful gusts of the wind. No doubt a walking holiday is the reason for their appearance along this road in the Dauphine Alps of France. Nothing out of the ordinary, nothing special. It is not even worth noting that they stroll out so early in the morning. Many walkers prefer this hour to enjoy the full beauty of the mountains. We might well forget them and so turn again to admire the lovely scene.

A glance back, just to see what the two travellers are now doing, is enough to convince us that something quite extraordinary is afoot.

1

Behind the two, where half a minute earlier shone the clear, morning light, is a huge, lumbering shape, a vast mass of apparently living matter. It must have come up the path as silently as a mouse and then into view while we were looking the other way. What can it be for a moment, the huge, black silhouette defies identification. But of course! There's nothing else it could be. It must be an elephant!

This is confirmed when it wheels into side view and reveals a long, mansized proboscis. The two gentlemen do not seem in the slightest perturbed. They apparently behave as if this is the same old early morning stroll we had at first assumed they were taking. They are almost immediately joined by four more silhouetted figures, and while two of the group hold a map up against the vast flank of the elephant to steady it, the others pore over the wind-torn piece of paper and after a discussion and the identification of several landmarks, the party moves off with its enormous, mobile landmark in tow.

As if this is not enough to surprise us for the time being, one of the party produces a book from his rucksack and, having opened it about half-way through, starts to read a short paragraph aloud. Everybody listens attentively. There is at least unity of purpose in this party. Could the book be a local mountaineer's guide or perhaps a geologist's manual of the Savoie Alps the party is too far away for us to hear all that they are saying. However, gusts of wind convey something of its sense. Undoubtedly, it runs as a narrative, a story of bygone days, of battles, tempests, and of mountain conflict. Perhaps these are historians but ... why, why, why the elephant There is discussion now. One fellow with a large, stiff covered notebook looks at his watch and calls out for "readings". Two members of the team stop and look at small hand instruments they carry. One of these is clearly an altimeter, for the shouted answer is "Four

2

thousand, five hundred feet" and the "Two and a quarter miles" which can be heard above the wind, might imply that the other is a pedometer. Now they are out of sight and the sheer fantasy of the fact that an elephant yes, a real elephant has just passed and graced a setting which in its own right is breathtaking and out of the ordinary, begins to sink in.

It is not very often that you find yourself in a really odd situation, a situation into which you have placed yourself by degrees and in seemingly natural, logical fashion. Then, suddenly, you look at yourself and it and exclaim in astonishment "How in the world did all this happen." If, for example, you set off for a walk over the mountains with an elephant and seven companions, it is inevitable that sooner or later you will wake up one morning, after a particularly restful night or feeling unusually perky due to the healthy, mountain air, and begin to think in this questioning way. It is not that you have been unable ' to see the wood for the trees' until now but rather that the wood is seen in an entirely new setting.

One such morning, we had made a reasonably early start and I walked ahead with Jimmy. Jimmy is from Singapore. To any outsider, he looked a man heavily overdressed in camera equipment, for it dangled in awe-inspiring circles around his periphery. To me, he was simply 'Expedition Photographer. After rounding a corner we waited for the others. Ahead lay our mountains of challenge, a rough track leading upward; behind walked an elephant, a gentle, lovable elephant in the pride of her youth. Down the valley were the Pressmen, hordes of them, with thousands of pounds' worth of camera equipment and pens poised to satisfy the curiosity of the millions who, at this very moment, may have been reading about what had happened to the elephant the day before. Fortunately, the Press travelled by car and so did not follow us up to this altitude along the narrow footpath. I turned to my companion, "Jimmy," I said, "can you tell me how under Heaven we came to be doing this ?" He did not answer. He had seen some- thing of interest and with professional care was picking the right camera to shoot it. Then, as he raised the instrument to his eye, a glance in my direction showed that he had heard. As the camera was being focused, his voice came out from behind it, "Goodness only knows! I suppose you ought to know best yourself it was your crazy idea anyway, but I'm having the time of my life." He clicked his camera and lowered it. The others had joined us. There is no need to say who was the biggest and most important of the others. She came softly to a halt. Our map told us where we were, forty-seven miles from our start and with another one hundred a d two to do; but I could go on and on speculating as to why. It was not as simple as all that.

I remembered a conversation in smoke-bound Birmingham last winter. How I remember that evening! It was as clear as if it had been yesterday. My friend had been sitting in ungainly fashion on a table, paper-strewn with engineering calculations. I had had my back to the window and my hands resting on the radiator in an effort to keep warm. An idea came as he talked. The same night, three letters left a still smoke-bound Birmingham for the sunnier climes of Geneva, Lyon and Turin. Each was addressed to a British Consul and asked an unusual question. "Do you know of an elephant ... who might be available ... this summer" No, that was not the beginning. The glorious summer of 1956 swung into the full vision of my mind's eye. A walking tour of the Alps with two men-friends and my sister, armed with Latin and Greek textbooks, a recent copy of the Alpine Journal, and a book Alps and Elephants, had proved one of the happiest holidays we had ever had; but even that was not the start to this adventure.

Perhaps the story had really begun back in Cambridge where a group of us had walked through the dim, lamplit quadrangle of St. John's College talking in amused tones of an intellectual and highly complex discussion which was going on between Sir Gavin de Beer, then Curator of the Natural History Museum, London and Dr. McDonald, Senior Tutor of Clare College, Cambridge. The argument concerned Roman History, Topography, Phenology, Geology, Zoology, and a number of other 'ologies' ! Perhaps that was why we students found the question so fascinating, because it had so many aspects and presented such stimulating, intellectual exercise.

ssh yes. Hannibal

I tilted my head slightly on one side, thought for a moment and then shook it. In my hand was a book by Polybius. It was a history book-but written many years ago about two thousand, one hundred to be more exact. No, the Cambridge discussions were certainly not the start to the matter. Not even our old friend, Polybius, can really claim to have been at the beginning of what eventually brought about our jaunt with an elephant. It is true that without him we would never have had enough information for the carrying through of our journey, nor Dr. McDonald and Sir Gavin anything on which to base their theories. It is true that without the Cambridge arguments we would never have had the 1956 Expedition, and if that were the case no amount of imaginative thinking, while trying to keep hands warm on cold November evenings in Birmingham, would have ended by sending letters to three Consuls, and the eventual trans-Alpine journey of an elephant!

Well, let's start at the beginning. There was a man called HANNIBAL.

CHAPTER II

Background I: The Story of a Great General

The name means 'Joy of Baal', the boy grew up 'The hope of Carthage', the man proved 'The fear of Rome." He was born into a world of ferment and bitter war and brought up in the very midst of it, under the banner of his father's army.

History repeats itself. The world of the third century B.C. was to all intents and purposes the Mediterranean Basin and, as today, this world held two conflicting ideals. Against the commercial culture of Semitic Carthage was ranged the rugged pattern of Roman domination. The people of Carthage, prosperous city on the north coast of Africa, had originally come from the Phoenician states of Tyre and Sidon in Palestine about six hundred years earlier. They were great and adventurous traders, their policy was daringly expansionist and they proved themselves powerful enough to stand up to any other nation who might challenge their maritime supremacy of the western Mediterranean. Rome had recently managed to forge a small federation of states in Central and South Italy, and now opposed Carthaginian power.

The first Punic War (264-241 BC) was a scuffie over Sicily and proved a partial victory to Rome. Carthage lost her sea supremacy and security, but was still able to develop influence and amass wealth in her colony of Southern Spain. Hamilcar Barca, her great leader and supreme military commander had further plans of combating Rome but he was to leave the commission to his son- in-law and four sons, 'the lion's brood', after his sudden death in

228 B.C. From that moment the amazing personality of his eldest boy, Hannibal, came into its own.

At an early age, he had asked his father if he might go with him on his Spanish campaign. This was permitted on condition that in the temple of the great god, Baal, he should stand in front of the Holy Sacrifice and swear eternal enmity to Rome. The memory of that scene, the small boy with his hand firmly clasped in his father's, must have remained with him for the rest of his life. Now, when he was nineteen, exactly ten years afterwards, that same father was killed in battle and handed on to him the commission to carry forward the flame of revenge.

But it was not for another ten years that he was able to turn his vow into full effect. Meanwhile, careful plans were in operation. At the early age of twenty-six Hannibal was unanimously chosen by the army to be their General. He proceeded to develop the Carthaginian hold on Spain. This was apparently to obtain sufficient money to pay back war debts to Rome, but, in reality, he realized that Spain was a bountiful source of manpower and supplies and would be an ideal base from which to attack. Has not this story a strangely modern flavour? In essence, Hannibal's aim was simple . . . nothing less than the utter destruction of Rome before Rome destroyed Carthage. It took a genius not only to spot the Achilles heel of his enemy but also to reach it. Hannibal perceived that Rome's weakest point was in Italy itself where the Federation of States was still loose and the cry of revolt sounded from the Celtic tribes of her north. He had now to get there. But how,

The Romans, however, thought there was little cause to fear a direct attack. Rome seemed impregnable. To the east, south and west lay the ocean, which she controlled. To the north lay the mighty fortress of the Alps, which not only presented great difficulties by its steepness, high altitude and areas of snow and ice but was also infested with mountain tribes, allied to Rome. They sat back, happy in illusory safety. No one would believe that Hannibal's army might attempt the 'impossible', that he could make the journey of fifteen hundred miles overland to Italy, crossing two great mountain ranges, passing through almost entirely hostile territory-but that is precisely what Hannibal had decided to do! So fearful were some of his men that one story tells of a fellow general suggesting to Hannibal that the men should be trained to eat their fellows in order to survive. It might have happened that his army would be known to posterity as 'Hannibal's Cannibals', but at least Hannibal never approved of the idea.

He captured the prosperous town of Saguntum on the Spanish coast and in 218 B.C., exactly ten years after his father's death, launched an avalanche which was to shake Rome to its very foundations. An army, well over ninety thousand strong, accompanied by a vast baggage train and a formidable herd of thirty-seven elephants, moving up the Mediterranean coast towards the Pyrenees was quite enough to send the Roman agents into a ferment of fear, and messengers scuttled to their ships to take the dread news to Italy. (A later chapter entitled 'Elephant' will explain why Hannibal brought these lumbering, food-consuming pachyderm.) The army consisted mainly of African and Spanish veterans but also contained men from many Mediterranean countries. Of the officers, two are worthy of note, for their interesting names! The director of the equivalent to our Royal Medical Corps was a surgeon called Synhalus who might well have been able to use his name in the commercial advertising of the day for a patent anti-cough inhalent !

The Field Prophet (Chaplain General) bore the interesting, and, to us, ignoble name of Bogus. I looked up the word in the dictionary, could only find it derives from the United States but I do suggest that someone there had been reading his ancient history! Having successfully crossed the Pyrenees, after much fighting and heavy losses, he made peace with a powerful Iberian state beyond and followed the coast road towards even more difficult obstacles. Between him and the mountains lay the fast-flowing river Rhone and he decided to attempt its crossing after four days' journey northwards from the sea. Hindrance and danger lay in three directions.

The swift, treacherous waters terrified the elephants, hostile Gauls lined the opposite bank and a Roman army was landing at the Rhone delta in a desperate bid to engage him in battle before he could attempt the Alps. It is a great tribute to his genius that all three difficulties were overcome; the first two by careful planning, forceful leadership and clever deception, and the last through speed of action. By the time Publius Scipio's forces arrived on the scene the Carthaginian army had been gone for three days.

The day after the Romans had decided to turn back and await the 'exhausted remains' of the army on the other side of the Alps, Hannibal came to a place on the Rhone called the 'Island'. Here a river called the 'Skaras' joined the main stream and formed a fertile triangle with a range of mountains on the third side. Having obtained lavish provisions from a friendly-king, his army, now reduced through desertion and death to thirty-six thousand foot soldiers and about ten thousand horse, followed the 'Skaras' for ten days before tackling the first piece of really Alpine country. The ensuing fortnight was the most tragic of the whole journey and it is the story of those fifteen days of struggle against almost insuper-able odds, which has stirred writers and thinkers for the last two thousand years. It is a story of terrible loss of life, of a courage and tenacity seldom equaled in die whole of history. Nearly two-fifths of that army was killed and the remainder, were described as being more like beasts than men by the time they made their final descent into Italy. Twice Hannibal was ambushed and the ponderous army suffered heavily at the hands of the hardy, Alpine tribes. Near the summit, the ascent and descent proved treacherous going as it was already late October and the fresh snow of autumn had settled on the hard slippery ice of the previous winter. There is little doubt that for several days, the men, horses and elephants literally starved. No wonder the mind of man boggles at the immensity of the task and weight of responsibility Hannibal had to bear. Our imagination is fired by a journey, the story of which will ever continue to echo down the corridors of time, and stirred in admiration for a general who not only led his forcess successfully over the Alps, down into the Po valley,' but thereupon was able to defeat the Romans in four great battles.

The first of these was fought in Northern Italy and took place only a short time after the arrival of his exhausted troops on to the plains. The other three, at Lake Trasimene, the rivers Trebia and Cannae, brought Hannibal to the verge of complete conquest over Rome. His military genius was shown to its finest advantage in a succession of brilliant strategies and unorthodox manreuvres. Cannae might well have sounded the death knell of Roman civilization; the Roman army of sixty thousand men was completely annihilated by a Carthaginian force which proved superior in every way, although only half the size. Hannibal's tactics at Cannae have never been surpassed or equalled.

But the tide had turned. With every disaster Rome's grim determination to survive increased and her Federation of States

remained unshaken. Hannibal continued to defeat one consular army after another, but with fewer than twenty thousand men and cut off entirely from his home country by the enemy-controlled sea, he was slowly being worn down. Interestingly enough, his life seems to have had its crises every ten years. It was in his tenth year that, before the gods and his father, he had sworn eternal enmity to Rome. Ten years after his early vow, his father had died. Ten more years led to his daring journey over the Alps and now, after a further decade of brilliant leadership against immense odds, he urgently called his brother, Hasdrubal, to come with reinforcements from

10

Spain. It was the turning point. Hasdrubal came but was completely defeated. The first news of the battle that Hannibal received was his brother's head, thrown into the camp by the Romans. He prophesied as he gazed into those sightless eyes, "I see there the fate of Carthage."

The end is sad. Hannibal left Italy, after fifteen years of campaigning, not because he was defeated but because Carthage had been attacked and needed his help. Even his military genius was not sufficient to reverse the position in Northern Africa. At the battle of Zama, Scipio Africanus defeated the Carthaginians, the war ended and as a measure of disarmament, elephants were for- bidden in the African stables. Nearly twenty years later, Hannibal committed suicide to avoid capture by Rome. He had been living the life of a soldier of fortune, continually fleeing from the revengeful Romans who could never forget Cannae, and assisting various small kingdoms of the Eastern Mediterranean in their local wars. He had proved himself a man of tremendous courage and audacity. There is little wonder that the phrase 'Hannibal ad Portas' (Hannibal is at the gates), was brought into the literature of Rome to galvanise the people into action whenever threatened by mortal danger.

There are a number of stories which cast light on Hannibal's character but one must not believe all of them. For instance, the statement by Appian that one winter in Lucania the Carthaginian general 'abandoned himself to unaccustomed luxury and the delights of love', has been shown to be mere Roman propaganda. On the contrary, Hannibal seems to have behaved with perfect propriety to his female captives and was a dutiful husband to Imilce, a lady of Greek descent who came from the Guadalquivir region in Spain.

He had wit too and could turn it to great account. By laughing uproariously with his lieutenant, Gisgo, just before Cannae, he broke the tenseness of the atmosphere and gave the soldiers confidence. A king proudly showed him his army which was about to engage the Romans. Hannibal's retort must have been most disconcerting: "Yes, it will be enough for the Romans, however greedy they may be."

His ingenuity was limitless and he is said to have invented biological warfare. While on his freelance travels, he assisted the King of Bithynia who was about to undertake a naval engagement against the King of Pergamun. Hannibal recommended throwing large earthenware jars of poisonous snakes on to the enemy ships when they came to close quarters. The jars broke, the snakes evidently caused much havoc and the victory was won !

His soldiers loved him, as we can see from the fact that for a fifteen-year campaign in enemy territory he was able so to bind together an army of Africans, Spaniards, Balearic Islanders, Ligurians, Gauls, Phoenicians, Italians and Greeks, that there is no record of discord amongst these varied peoples. Perhaps we may think that Livy's description of him as fearless and utterly prudent in danger, indefatigable, able to endure heat or cold, controlled in his eating habits, unpretentious in his dress and willing to sleep wrapped in a military cloak and lying among the outposts of his soldiers, a superb rider and horseman who prided himself on his care of his weapons and horses-is an over-glorification of a by then legendary figure, until we are told in the same chapter that he was inhumanly cruel, full of deception, having no reverence for sacred things or the gods and did not keep his oaths.

It is difficult to discover the truth about a figure grown legendary through the years, so feared by his enemies and so admired by his friends. One thing is certain, however. Hannibal is undoubtedly one of the greatest generals in history. To him we pay our tribute.

CHAPTER III

Background II: The Story of an Investigation

TOGETHER WITH THE stories of his exploits, Hannibal has left behind him a riddle. The appeal and fascination of that riddle is in direct relation to the greatness of his achievement-the crossing of the mighty barrier of the Alps. Why and when he crossed is clear but the oft-repeated question "Where did he cross?" has been asked right down through history. The problem is in the best tradition of detective stories. Indeed, it can be considered one of the earliest of these passed down to us. Many people have been irresistibly lured into investigation and during the last two thousand years, historians, classicists, generals, mountaineers, parsons, politicians and even an emperor have fallen easy prey to the strange fascination of the question. Here is a detective story of the highest calibre, of the strangest enticement, the kind of problem that will keep you sitting up late in bed when you should have been asleep long ago.

The investigation of, say, a murder can be split up into three separate stages though their order can vary. The detective would set out to:

(One) Obtain as full a story as possible from those in any way connected with the case.

(Two) With this information in mind, to study the ground and setting of the crime and then to re-examine the evidence given by the witnesses.

(Three) Consider the conclusions of others (if any) who have already investigated the case.

From these he is able to formulate his own conclusions. Here is the only logical method to tackle the 'Hannibal' problem and the same stages occur.

STAGE ONE. Studying the ancient records, assessing their relative importance and amassing a number of criteria

The Alpine crossing has been recorded by several classical writers but most fully by Polybius and Livy. Modern scholarship has shown that Polybius is by far the most reliable source of information. His life overlapped Hannibal's by twenty years, he had ample opportunity of meeting those who had fought in the war and he obtained first-hand information about the crossing from Silenos, a Greek who survived the terrible journey over the Alps and put the story on paper. (Unfortunately this account has not been preserved.) Polybius himself claims to have traversed the Alps in Hannibal's footsteps only sixty years after the event, to check up on the details. He was a fine military historian with unbiased outlook and a brilliant mind. He recounts the details of the journey with such vividness and control that one cannot but believe that he obtained his story from an eyewitness.

Livy lived a hundred and fifty years later, was a friend of the Emperor Augustus and set himself the enormous task of writing a history of Rome. His approach was not nearly so precise and accurate and he used a scissors-and-paste technique which incorporated the writings of Polybius and others. Hence there are times when he contradicts himself and exaggerates. He lived in an era when already men had began to speculate about the route so that in sections one feels that he is writing his or someone else's theory and not the unbiased facts. However, his account gives details, which add vividly to the story.

Other writers, such as Varro, Strabo and Cornelius Nepos, have mentioned Hannibal and a considerable amount can be learnt through cross-checking their stories with those of Livy and Polybius.

If the detective in you now sorts out the clues to the mystery from the various stories of these early 'witnesses', the following· would seem to be the major factors to bear in mind when you eventually set out to explore the ground.

Note: Those already mentioned in Chapter II are only lightly mentioned. The Roman unit of measurement is the stade (1 mile = 9.1 stades).

Factors

(1) The character and, particularly, the audacity of Hannibal.

(2) The size of his army, its character and composition. Don't forget the 37 elephants.

(3) The types of elephants and their uses (see Chapter XVIII).

(4) The typical marching speed of the army in varying altitudes and terrain. This is where our elephant came in useful (see Chapter XVIII).

(5) The time of year: late October; at the setting of the Pleiades, hence there was fresh snow on the ground.

(6) The number of days Hannibal took to cover the distances between the key landmarks.

(a) From the Mediterranean to the crossing of the Rhone; four days for Hannibal, three for the Romans under Scipio. This shows that Hannibal must have left the coast road before coming to the Rhone delta.

(b) From the crossing to the 'Island'; four days (600 stades—which is about 70 miles).

(c) From the 'Island' to the 'Ascent towards the Alps;' ten days (800 stades—which is about 90 miles). Hannibal must have spent at least the first two or three days of the ten at the Island, getting provisions.

(d) From the 'Ascent' to the enemy town, two days of fighting (through a point of ambush).

(e) Having taken it, he rests at the enemy town for one day.

(f) From this town to the place where tribes meet him and pretend to be friendly; three days.

(g) From this place to the 'Bare Rock'; two days (scene of second ambush).

(h) From 'Bare Rock' to the Summit Pass; one day. (Total: nine days.)

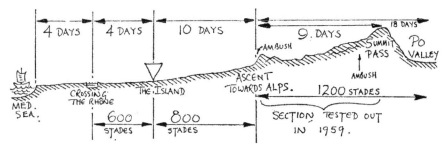

(i) Rest on the summit; two days.

(j) Hannibal getting elephants past narrow dangerous section; four days.

(k) From here to the flat country; three days. Total: eighteen days, from the 'Ascent' to the Plains of Italy.

(7) Not only is it necessary for each landmark to fit into correct relative position as shown above but also, to satisfy a detailed description.

(a) The crossing of the Rhone lies where the river is a single stream, flows extremely fast and the surrounding tribes have many boats.

(b) The Island: The size and shape of the Nile Delta with two rivers, the 'Skaras' and the Rhone forming two sides and a range of high mountains the third, extremely fertile and prosperous.

(c) The 'Ascent towards the Alps.' The first stretch of really mountainous country, not necessarily over a pass (but through a gorge), ideal for an ambush, in the area of the Allobrogians.

(d) The 'Enemy town'-within easy reach of the gorge, rich and prosperous. (Hannibal found provisions for three days.)

(e) Place of meeting with the tribes-at the beginning of a new district or in a town.

(f) The 'Bare Rock'-a place ideal for an ambush, with steep cliff faces and a position on a cliff-surrounded promontory from which Hannibal could have defended the advance of his pack-train.

(g) The Summit Pass (the most important place to locate) must:

(i) be large enough to camp 30,000 men and about 5,000 horses (on its western side),

(ii) command a panoramic view of the Po valley,

16

(iii) have a difficult descent,

(iv) be high enough to have large areas of snow from two consecutive winters on its flanks,

(v) have a place for pasturing the horses immediately after the difficult stretch of the descent,

(vi) give a distance of three days' march, to the plains,

(vii) lead straight down into the land of the Turini,

(viii) be a day's march from a probable site of the 'bare rock' ambush (or a day and a night for the baggage and elephants),

(ix) be positioned so that the most direct route to it from the Rhone passes by the 'Island' (where the river 'Skaras' meets the Rhone), seven days march from the sea. (Three days from the sea to the crossing of the Rhone and four from the crossing to the Island.)

STAGE TWO. Studying the ground

When a murder has been discovered it goes without saying that as much as possible is left in the exact position and condition in which it was found. The detective, on arrival, will have to start investigating the ground and build up a picture of what it was like at the time of the crime. This ground would not normally involve a vast area. But the area to be considered in the 'Hannibal problem' stretches for hundreds of square miles of mountainous terrain and incorporates innumerable passes leading from east to west. These lie on a continuous ridge, running northwards and then curving westwards from the Mediterranean.

However, the situation is not as difficult as it might at first appear. On studying the formation of the Alps, it can be seen that two major valleys penetrate it from the east, those of the Isere and the Durance rivers, and it is almost certain that Hannibal used either one or the other to climb up into the highest regions. Branching off from the Isere valley runs the curving valley of the river Arc which also could lead an army up towards the frontier range. Hence there are three possible routes:

(a) A northern route, following the Isere right up to the Little Saint Bernard Pass.

(b) A central route, following the Isere and then forking off up the Arc river to the Mount Cenis-Clapier passes.

(c) A southern route, following the Durance basin, from where it flows into the Rhone or via the Isere or Drome rivers- this leads to the passes of Mont Genevre, Scalla, Bousson, Traversette and Larche.

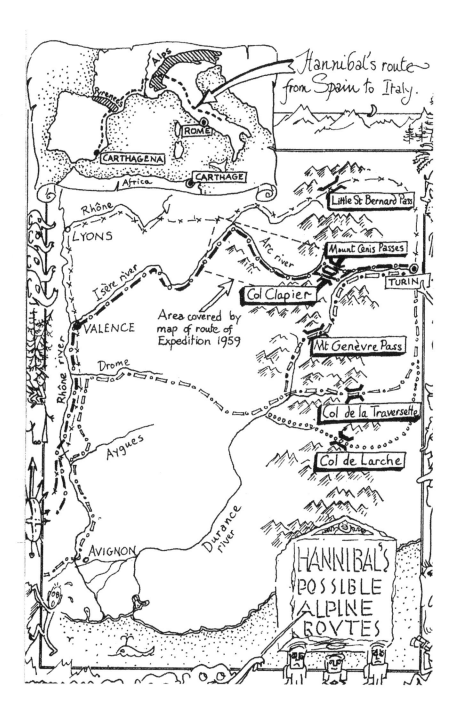

Hannibal's route from Spain to Italy.

Alps

Pyrenees

ROME

CARTHAGENA

CARTHAGE

Africa

Rhône

LYONS

Arc river

Little St Bernard Pass

Mount Cenis Passes

TURIN

Col Clapier

Isère river

VALENCE

Area covered by map of route of Expedition 1959

Mt Genèvre Pass

Rhône river

Drome

Col de la Traversette

Aygues

Col de Larche

Durance river

AVIGNON

HANNIBAL'S POSSIBLE ALPINE ROUTES

STAGE THREE: Considering the conclusions of others

Few problems have received so much attention from the questioning minds of the world. Napoleon thought Hannibal used the central route, along the Isere and Arc. One of the earliest recorded theories is that of Josias Simler who in 1574 postulated the use of either a Mont Cenis or Mont Genevre route. Before me lie seven learned tomes, each putting forward, in convincing terms with clear scholarly argument, different theories as to Hannibal's way I, personally, feel William John Law, M.A. (of Christ Church, Oxford), beats the lot. In 1866 he produced two weighty volumes, each containing a vast amount of careful, painstaking reasoning in which he devotes one complete section, consisting of four chapters, solely to 'The Authority of Polybius'. He dedicates the mammoth work to his grandfathers, the Bishop of Carlisle and the Arch- bishop of York, 'sincere lovers of truth'. There is no doubt that men have taken the problem with extreme seriousness.

But do not imagine that the question is of interest only to men. Though women have not written about it, their views are held with just as much vehemence and dogmatism. I remember three years ago sitting beside a typical peasant woman on a French bus. Somehow we started to talk and the subject came round to Hannibal. When she heard that I doubted the Traversette theory, I thought she would move to another seat in disgust ! She was adamant that Hannibal had used Traversette. There was no other pass in the running! She talked about it all as if Hannibal had crossed the Alps only a few years ago and as if the route he took affected her personal welfare. This was by no means a rare case.

Go into any cottage or tavern in Hannibal country and you will be able to have a discussion on the question. The stimulating and sometimes heated controversy has gone on for hundreds of years.

Modern scholarship has been brought to bear on the problem and Sir Gavin de Beer, former Curator of the Natural History Museum, London, Dr. McDonald, Senior Tutor of Clare College, Cambridge, and Dr. de Lavis-Trafford, a leading authority on the Maurienne Alps, have all published works on Hannibal within the last four years. As we progress in the investigation we will consider their conclusions, together with those of earlier writers and use these to guide our thinking when we finally make up our mind.

For the last two thousand years investigation had ended at Stage

Three. Stage Four is entirely novel in this context. It is to demonstrate, by actual experiment, the practicability of a hypothesis. This we intended to do ... with an elephant!

CHAPTER IV

Cambridge Carthaginians, 1956

(Stages One, Two and Three)

I was in my final year at Cambridge. Life had become a hectic rush to prepare for final Tripos examinations. To make it worse the college seemed full of coffee-drinking friends who insisted that you should go out with them, to continue amongst other things that 'sadly interrupted talk on metaphysics'. Such people are clearly unsympathetic to examinees. "My dear fellow," was the despairing cry, "do you realise that there are only four weeks to Tripos and I have at least eight weeks' work to do before then!"

No wonder many of us neglected any thought for the future life after the examinations-even those who were reasonably confident of passing. Someone might raise the subject at dinner in Hall but the others would visibly cower away and hastily change the subject. The problems of the present were far too pressing- but we longed for release! For me, an engineering student, the great world of industry lay as a hungry dragon, ready to swallow up in one gulp the gracious living of college days; but somehow I managed to force myself to face reality. After I had been interviewed by several firms I promptly tried to forget them and hurried back to my slide rule.

The reason why one lovely summer's evening we started to talk about Hannibal's route over the Alps was probably that we were all exhausted by study and only too pleased to find a new topic of conversation that was neither work, careers or jobs. Moreover, we discovered in it a strange fascination, which had already begun to stimulate our examination-stunted faculties of thought. The suggestion was that a group should look for Hannibal's route that very summer. We did not progress beyond this point that evening but the germ of the idea was planted.

Examinations had now ended. The leisure of Cambridge life was ours to enjoy-punting, tennis, long coffee parties; even metaphysics and who would have guessed it Hannibal! A group of us started to read the early writers and the conflicting views of Dr. McDonald, and Sir Gavin de Beer. There seemed no more logical step to take than to go and see how these arguments fitted in with the actual terrain of 'Hannibal Country'. There and then the Cambridge Hannibal Expedition was formed and quickly went into action.

There were four of us; Richard Jolly who had just taken a first-class degree in Economics at Magdalene College; David Jenkins, a second-year Theologian, also from Magdalene; my sister Elizabeth and myself, then at St. John's College. Organisation was simple. The main condition of membership was at least a dawning understanding of the problem and enthusia. Our reading became extensive and we circulated a wide variety of books. Friends would look nonplussed when, having rushed in to persuade the newly initiated Hannibalian to play tennis, they found his nose deep in a copy of Polybius. Moreover, the nose would not budge and someone else had to be found to make up the foursome.

At that stage in our experience the Col de Clapier, supported by Dr. McDonald, and the Col de la Traversette, by Sir Gavin de Beer seemed the two of most importance, though I now consider the passage over the Col de Mont Genevre has an equally strong, if not stronger, claim as Traversette. It was simplest to have two passes in mind, each connected with the name of a famous modem scholar; and although we passed over all three, we mainly studied Clapier and Traversette. If you have read Chapter III carefully, you will have no difficulty in guessing what kind of landmark we were searching for. The pass itself would be of most interest. Here we could try to discover the scene described so graphically by Polybius-the view of the Po valley, the altitude, the steepness of descent and ascent, the amount of ground available for camping. Vie wanted to study all these; sketch, photograph and then compare them. Working back from the pass, we would have to locate the bare rock, the enemy village, the ascent towards the Alps, the Island, and finally the crossing of the Rhone.

Mentally our problem was a magnificent stimulant, a pleasant change from working out questions on moments of inertia of 'complex bodies', so popular in my Mechanics examination. Now we could turn to the problem of the reason for the inertia of Hannibal's complex bodies, his elephants, when he wanted them to cross the Rhone. Yes, obviously our summer holiday was going to be extremely worthwhile, and quite different from anything we had experienced up till then.

The few weeks before going down from Cambridge and setting out on our investigation quickly filled themselves with necessary preparation details. Next to Carthage itself, the best place for mental acclimatisation was the British Museum. Here I sat, gazing at ancient Carthaginian carvings and speculating on the background life of the 'greatest enemy of Rome'. Permission was granted for the expedition to visit the Mecca of Britain's coin collecting in the eastern wing of the museum. Security was strict. Having had the great doors slammed behind us and locked firmly, we had to sign special forms in an ante-room. Then we were shown to a long, low table and brought priceless Carthaginian coins on quaint, wooden trays. Some dated back to the very time of Hannibal and one bore the magnificent figure of an African elephant, almost certainly one of the general's. We fingered these carefully, with the reverence due to the name of Hannibal. No one minded being locked in with all this!

Having learnt Sir Gavin de Beer's book, Alps and Elephants, practically off by heart I thought it wise to write to its author, who had provided us with such useful and controversial information. The reply reaffirmed his Crusading spirit of support for the Theory of Traversette, and showed kind interest in our plans. He seemed doubtful, however, that we would find another pass out of the Durance Basin which would fulfil the conditions laid down by Polybius. Unfortunately, as Sir Gavin was out of the country at the time, we were unable to meet him and discuss the problems.

We did meet Dr. McDonald, however, the defender of the Col de Clapier route, one sunny midday at the Cambridge Arts Rooftop

24

Restaurant. He, too, was pleased to hear of our project. We spent a gay hour talking what can only be described as 'Hannibal Language '. Richard and I walked away feeling we had come into contact with a real expert in the game. He had infused us with a new desire for deeper understanding of the problem. Moreover, his theories seemed convincing. He knew what he was talking about and, in each aspect of the matter, reached the core of the problem in a few deft sentences. So, armed with all the necessary books and our rucksacks piled high with ancillary equipment, we left England.

We were to visit Clapier first. Wednesday, the 22nd August passed in a blaze of sunshine, and its evening saw the miniature expedition safely settled into a barn at Bramans. This high-altitude village stands at the junction of two important valleys. One leads the main road from Modane towards the Col de Mont Cenis. The other winds upwards for twenty kilometres to the Col de Clapier. Hence, its position is strategic. I stood now at the crucial fork of the road, with the chill night, wind blustering down upon the few huddled roofs of Bramans and the old barn door creaking heavily. I pictured the great forms of elephants lumbering steadily upwards in the shadows of the night, the creak of harness and the shouts of Carthaginian mahouts. I imagined the discussion that went on at Bramans and the final decision to take the short cut over Clapier. The burning torches, shouts and tramp of feet faded into the shadows and my torch led me back into the barn where the others were already asleep.

Next day we climbed to Le Planey, which would be the assault camp from which to reach Col de Clapier. This tiny outpost of civilisation stands on the very edge of an awe-inspiring, treeless land known only to the chamois, marmot and occasional climber a land of mist and bitter winds, of jagged peaks and eternal snows. We watched the setting sun flooding the mountain crags all around us with vivid red, and energetically dubbined our boots in keen anticipation.

It is difficult to convey our initial disappointment next day as the clouds hung low and a gentle drizzle discouraged our plans for an early start. Our disappointment proved transitory for the weather began to improve. We climbed rapidly, the weather was fairly cold but the effort of carrying our heavy packs kept· us warm. In twenty-five minutes we met our 'guides', two frontier gendarmes whom we had by good fortune come across the previous day. From them we had obtained the necessary permission to cross the frontier by the usually forbidden Col de Clapier route. A smile and a joke had won where many a letter to Consuls had failed.

They now led the way as we zigzagged up the left-hand side of the valley; behind us were snow-capped peaks, on our right; a gorge curving towards the magnificent Ambin Glacier, ahead, emerging on either side, steep ramparts of cloud-obscured peaks. After an hour and a half, climbing was over and our trek continued on more level ground, the scenery being a strange mixture of deserted planet and the odd tin-can evidence of civilisation. At one point we passed four broken-down huts. These were of vital, strategic importance in our planning for the elephant assault. As we neared the pass, at 8,173 feet above sea level, the grass wore to a thin finish, the snowdrifts came down to our level and the gale gusts grew stronger. Suddenly we were there, looking down a steep valley to the Italian foothills. As the ranges faded into the distance, far beyond them, through the haze of a summer midday, could be seen the plains of Po. It was a great thrill to imagine Hannibal standing on this very spot encouraging his exhausted men and pointing them down to the 'promised land'. Though it was apparently extremely hot in the valley, the chill wind which tore at our jackets permitted us only to take some convincing photographs of the Italian view and surrounding peaks, and then brusquely pushed us off our high, ledge-like vantage point down on to the steep, ankle-straining path, which zigzagged towards the tree-line, far below us. After spending the night in a most hospitable monastery up in the mountains, we climbed down to Susa, a town right at the base of the Alps on the

Italian side. We had finished our study of the Clapier route.

A series of generous motorists enabled the Expedition to forge its way back over the Col de Mont Genevre into France. It was now on the southern section of its investigation, and determined to see something of Sir Gavin de Beer's route leading up to the Col de la Traversette, a pass over a thousand feet higher than the Col de Clapier.

While on the Mont Genevre pass, we noted several things. Its altitude is low (only 6,083 feet above sea-level), it commands no panoramic view and, right from Roman times, has been considered an easy pass. On the other hand, there is plenty of room for an army to camp and one part of the descent could have given considerable difficulty if covered by ice and snow.

Assault camp for the Traversette was the deserted village of L'Echalpe. Misfortune seemed to have doomed this tiny hamlet to a most desolate existence for not only had it been gutted during the last war, but it had also been struck by avalanche and flood. Our arrival caused quite a stir, for the total population (the last two families brave enough to live there) turned out in force to see the newcomers. We made friends well enough and David and Richard went off with a wizened old farmer to get hay for our beds while Elizabeth and I made ready the ruined, but at least roofed, school-house for camping. You could not imagine an eerier place. Stealthy gusts of wind crept along the deserted lanes and past our hideout, creaking the broken-down shutters and scattering the leaves. A waterpipe dripped continually outside and would change its note when caught up in the wind. We huddled more closely around the two remaining candles and ate our primitive supper.

Next morning we made an early start and found the ascent as exciting as that to Clapier. Here, the easier part of the climb came first. Towards the end, where it crossed a large area of rock scree, the going became uneven and steep. At times we thought we had lost our way, for the path would disappear in a mass of stony land- slide. However the sharp edge of a frontier ridge lay to our left and we made for this. Up and up the climb took us until at last we came to what might have been the edge of a giant volcanic crater, or the very brink of Hell itself Here was the Col de la Traversette 9,760 feet above sea-level, a mere fifteen yards across, with steep sides which one could literally straddle. The French slopes were bathed in sunshine. All that could be seen of Italy was a vast, dynamic wall of dense mist, racing upwards in wild, futile gestures as if conveying the desperate struggles of those in Hades beneath. We peered over what seemed to us to be a sheer edge and could dimly discern dark, jagged rocks sloping downwards. A little refuge gave shelter from the winds as we opened rucksacks, munched lettuce, tomatoes, tinned meat and apples, and waited for the mist to clear. It did, and revealed a magnificent view, even more panoramic than that from Clapier. Far over to the right reared the superb peak of Mont Viso, cloaked in its eternal snows and with a vast flag of mist, streaming from its leeward side.

Our imagination almost boggled at the picture of Hannibal on the knife-edge pass. If he had gone this way the ascent and descent would indeed have been terrible. We made a careful study of the setting, altitude, steepness, places where there must have been landslides since Hannibal's day, the area for camping, view, and so on, and climbed down to the valley that evening, feeling completely awe-inspired by the fantastically majestic landscape that had surrounded us all day, and a good deal wiser in our study of Hannibal's route. The valuable information in our log-book was beginning to mount up and we had already started to formulate opinions. Moreover, over a hundred photographs of the passes, and possible locations for the 'bare rock' where Hannibal lost so many men and pack-horses were being sent off for development as we left for an entirely different sphere of investigation-the Rhone valley.

We had an adventurous and valuable experience when we went to see, study and photograph the points where Sir Gavin and Dr. McDonald place Hannibal's crossing of the river and the 'Island'. The climax came when a two-day lift in an oil-tanker chugging up the Rhone made this close investigation immediately possible and gave time for thought. During those days we discussed a multitude of subjects including pacifism, politics and the colour question. Furthermore, the team was able to catch up on its daily study of St. Luke's Gospel, which had been getting rather behind- hand. Our holiday was proving a period of immense spiritual value. Through seeking Hannibal we had begun to discover our- selves and each other. Never have I enjoyed such complete concord and openness of heart with others as then.

"Come on, Richard. You're the man for the job." It was Elizabeth's voice. We were sitting in a waterlogged tent, an extension of the

Youth Hostel at Valence, trying to keep dry, and winding up the affairs of the expedition. Next day its members would be going their several ways. We had decided that it would be a good idea to write an article about the marvellous time we had had. Who was to write it? Richard, of course. The rest of us unanimously agreed. He was not quite so sure-but that didn't matter. It was three against one so the question was settled.

"Now what would you like me to write about?" he asked. "Oh, start off with something of human interest," I said casually. "I suppose there would be enough just on the different types of transport we have used to keep you busy for a month of

Sundays. Let's list them aeroplane, car, lorry, oil-tanker, bicycle, cable car, railway, foot — "

"Oh, shut up, John," Richard chirped in with a twinkle in his eye. "What we want is something academic-after all, we have been following Hannibal's route." He adopted a sterner approach: "Now, David, what have you learnt from this expedition, academically speaking?"

Over came the thoughtful reply: "Well, for one thing, it seems as if even Polybius-our dear, dependable Polybius—exaggerates quite happily. For instance, where are the range of mountains almost inaccessible and difficult to climb or penetrate' on the third side of the 'island'? I can't find them!"

"Look here," I said. "Before we decide what to say, how about deciding for whom we are to write this. Do you think the Tele- graph would take it?"

"Doubt it! The Manchester Guardian is a more likely bet." There was general agreement, it being felt that our extraordinary little cocktail of historical investigation and gay, student adventure would be best suited to Guardian readers.

Elizabeth wanted to summarise our findings as briefly as possible.

"Would you say these were our conclusions? Because Polybius provides a more exact description of Hannibal's pass than of any other part on his route, we have concentrated our investigation on that point i"

"Quite correct."

"Well then, we favour the Col de Clapier to the Col de la

Traversette—"

"Wait a minute," broke in Richard who had been scribbling in his notebook, and then he looked up. "We ought to say why we have chosen these two passes out of all the many."

"Because they are the only two which give a good view of the Po valley," David said.

"And also because they have such strong protagonists in the persons of Sir Gavin de Beer and Dr. McDonald. After all, they both, put forward very convincing arguments for their theories," I added.

Elizabeth went on, and she stared up at the leaking tent roof as she thought aloud: "We see that both passes could be considered high enough to have the snow of two consecutive winters, both have a steep and difficult descent, both give a good view, but"- there was a pause-" to my mind, two points tell against Sir Gavin—"

I broke in, for brothers are always allowed to be rude! "For one thing, there is no room on or near his pass to camp three hundred men, let alone thirty thousand."

"It's not only that, but the climb up to Traversette was fantastically difficult. Sir Gavin argues that landslides have made the way more difficult, but if anything I would say that they should have created a gradient more shallow than it was in 218 BC"

Richard remarked: "If only we could challenge him to take an elephant over !"

"If he did, it would die and we would prove our point," David concluded.

I broke in: "My strongest criticism of Traversette is that it does not lead down into the country of the Turini. It is a good fifty kilometers too far south. Clapier satisfies this condition perfectly." "All the same," said David, "although Clapier looks likely, it beats me why Hannibal should go traipsing all the way up the sere and then the Arc to reach Italy when he could easily have taken the Durance route to the Col de Mont Genevre and crossed with relative ease.

"But that just doesn't fit in with the conditions. For one thing, Genevre does not give a good view of the Po valley. Moreover, it is so jolly low and is more than three days' journey from the plains of Italy. Anyway, if you choose a Durance route, as Sir Gavin has done, you get stuck on the lower section of the journey. The positioning of the Island has to be pushed so far south that we get the ridiculous position of having Hannibal travel at fourteen kilometres a day along the easy Rhone valley when he is being chased by the Romans and then twenty kilometres a day on much more difficult ground. An Isere 'Island' fits in so much better."

David was keen to get back to the human side of the story. "Now the Guardian won't want just academic mumbo jumbo. Richard, tell them about how we came to stay in that Italian monastery and of the beautiful singing there."

"And of the old woman in a bus who swears Hannibal dug a tunnel under Traversette."

"And of ... "

A month later I was in Birmingham, for I had actually been accepted by one of those firms I was telling you about at the beginning of the chapter. A scribbled postcard arrived, in Richard's writing. 'Guardian turned it down, Said it fell between two stools. So I sent it higher-read The Times, boy!"

I hurried over to a bookstall, bought a copy and then went in search of my favourite armchair. Having satisfied my demand for comfort, I turned to the central page. There in bold lettering at the head of a full two-column article stood the words: by our Special Correspondent.

CHAPTER V

Birth of an Expedition

OVER TWO YEARS had passed since then and to all intents and purposes the ghosts of Hannibal and his elephants were well and truly buried. Admittedly, a further reconaissance patrol, this time to the Pyrenees, had been made to see where the Carthaginians might have crossed. Admittedly, the opportunities to lecture on our own enthusiastic quest in Britain, with the Foyle's Lecture Agency, and abroad, with the Foreign Office and British Council, proved that the appetite of an international public had been whetted. But, nevertheless, where could we go from here? We had stated our findings, and as the many and more illustrious men who had gone before had done, we could leave yet another piece of literature to add to the ever mounting collection.

Somehow, I was dissatisfied. After all, ours was just a theory and as such probably seemed no more convincing than any of the others. Did it bear the mark of sound reasoning and scholarly thought? Would it stand the passage of time? Sir Gavin had given an excellent illustrated talk on television, even demonstrating how Hannibal could have split the rock with vinegar. Since that day the British public seemed convinced that Traversette was Hannibal's path. We disagreed; but what could we do? It was just a matter of one theory vying against another.

A further reading of Polybius and Livy started a train of thought. Their story rests on a day-to-day itinerary account so that any calculation of the route turns not on miles so much as days' travel as affected by the topography. If the route of Hannibal were to be tested out with a modern army and herd of elephants, calculations would have to be based, not of an average day's speed, but of distance covered by army and elephants in the conditions which Hannibal found on any one particular day. Much as we would like to see the opposing armies of the world unite to make a peaceful time-distance study over the mountains, and an alliance of European Zoos and circuses to provide a suitably formidable herd of elephant for our purposes, the chances of international statesmen agreeing to co-operate on the project seemed rather remote.

I lay in bed one night unable to sleep. Could we not take one elephant over? Yes, take it along the Clapier route from the 'Ascent towards the Alps' to the summit pass. The time-distance study would still be valid, even though not as realistic as with an army. If we could make careful measurement of our elephant's relative speeds at different altitudes, and road surface, the comparative results could be brought to bear on our theory and would indicate whether we really were justified in placing the' Ascent' at Pontcharra, the 'enemy town' at La Rochette, the 'bare rock' at L'Esseillon and finally, the pass at the Col de Clapier. After all, were the distances between these points practicable in the time given ? Going by the speed of the elephant Richard Halliburton had ridden over the Great St. Bernard Pass in 1937, it seems that unacclimatised elephants are seriously affect d by altitude at over 6,000 feet above sea-level. Was this really so ? How do elephants react to this kind of condition ? Halliburton's just refused to move.

Surely Hannibal's were better climbers. 'But even if you do think it a good idea to perform a practical study with an elephant,' I said to myself, 'where are you going to get one from ... for no one will risk hiring one out let alone lending it. Who would insure it? How would you supply its food? Who would provide the money?"

I lay in bed thinking around the problem. It was well after midnight but I just couldn't sleep. All I had was an idea-just an idea, a flimsy ghost craft tossed hither and thither on the tempestuous sea of my mind. It was so fragile that it might well fall to pieces and be blown away before morning. I awoke and it was still intact.

Exactly eight months later, to the day, our Channel ferry was butting its way through the rough seas to France. This was real! —

and the misty coastline of Normandy over to our starboard was real too ! A group of adventurers were on their way to meet an elephant and then walk with her over the Alps.

CHAPTER VI

Preparations

THE FEW REMAINING months before we began our journey in the French Alps were crammed with countless things to do. Here was a challenge which demanded every ounce of our energy, ever facet of our imagination and every tortuous turn of our ingenuity.

Of the original team, neither David nor Elizabeth was available in the summer. That left two of us to try to bring our dream to reality. Richard had just come back from two years as a District Officer in Kenya and was now at Magdalene College, Cambridge, busy with a post-graduate course in economics. As I was a hundred miles away, in Birmingham, deep in a production engineering job our problems of communication and planning were enormous.

If I were writing a do-it-yourself manual on *How to Take An Elephant Over the Alps* I might try to make out that it was an easy exercise. But I am not, and I will omit any mention of the word 'easy'. The business is not simple, and it is almost impossible if you try, as we did, to keep our preparations secret. Consider the complications involved even in the first stage.

STAGE ONE: *Find an Elephant* ... and make sure it is the right colour.

We launched a three-pronged attack by sending letters of inquiry to the British Consuls in Lyons, Geneva and Turin, as these were the nearest places of importance to our planned journey. I must admit my lack of faith; for there were voices in my mind whispering monotonously that we had not a dog's chance of obtaining what we wanted.

The miracle had happened. I held in my hand a letter from Turin, with the promise of a real, live, two-and-a-half ton elephant. Was there more than coincidence in this ? On the very day that our letter had arrived, La Stampa, leading newspaper of Turin, carried the news that a bonny, young pachyderm was looking for an owner. Signor Arduino Terni, Director of the Turin, Milan and Varallo Sesia Zoos, bought and then offered her to us on loan for the projected journey. Moreover, Jumbo, for that was her name, would be available free of charge and with a mahout provided! There was no turning back now. The expedition was 'on' !

STAGETWO: Find an Alp

This we had, fortunately. It was just about all we did have at the first but still it was something. As soon as we knew that Jumbo was available I wrote to Dr. McDonald and told him all about our dreams and plans. He replied immediately with the now famous words 'Delighted to hear you have an elephant-a necessary thing, like the Scot finding a golf ball to start the game', and supported the venture with great enthusiasm. We were delighted when he accepted the presidency of the expedition. Sir Gavin also showed great interest. He suggested dryly in one letter that our elephant should be a specimen of the Cyclotis variety of Loxodonta Africana from south of the Gambia river.

We were to start at Montmelian, in the Savoie Alps of France, and cover the one hundred and sixty miles over the frontier to Turin.

STAGE THREE. Get the elephant insured

This was by no means an easy task. I have calculated that I must have spent at least the equivalent of two and a half full weeks, with an average eight-hour day (in the evenings and week-ends) on this subject alone. Evidently, Lloyd's had been known to insure elephants on unusual ventures such as ours, so to them I would go. But to whom, in that vast organisation ? I happened to be in London for the day, seeing the Curator for Mammals at the London Zoo about elephant boots, so decided to start proceedings with a telephone call.

My fingers apprehensively flipped over the pages of the directory. L-ah. Ll—oh yes, that's right. Lloyds. Here we are. Now which number out of this formidable list are you going to choose ? Lloyds of London had a whole battery of offices. I made a guess and dialed carefully, with a twinkle in my eye. This was going to be fun!

" Hullo, is that Lloyds ?"

"Yes, can I help you, sir ?" It was a girl's voice (obviously that of a secretary). Was I to break the news to her, the news we had so jealousy guarded from the Press I Could I trust her ? I should have foreseen this long ago. How ridiculous to expect to be straight away put into contact with a confiding, high-powered executive.

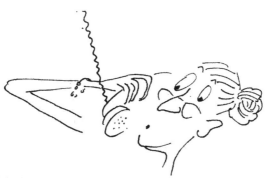

Would she believe me ? Obviously not. I started to hedge. "Could you put me through to the right department ? I want to insure the passage of a large animal over the Alps."

"What sort of large animal ?" Clearly, here was a very persistent young lady. Did they really have different departments to insure different types of large animals over the Alps ?

"Well, its an ... its an elephant. An elephant over the Alps," I said it firmly, almost as if I was trying to persuade myself that this was so.

There was silence and then an extraordinary noise-half-way between a scream and a giggle. A loud knock indicated that the receiver had peen hastily dropped and more distant, feminine sounds could be heard. The whole of the office seemed buzzing with consternation. A further pause and distant muttering. Ah, the receiver had been picked up now but there was silence at the other end. Suddenly, a new feminine voice spoke with firmness." Excuse me, sir, my friend did not quite hear what you said. Would you repeat it ?"

"I want to insure an elephant for a walk over the Alps," I shouted from my end and raised myself off my heels as if unconsciously trying to attain the height of this new lady. Obviously she was tall, probably thin, certainly middle-aged and an extremely efficient head of the department. Her voice came back as if she had handled this kind of problem all her life. "I presume you will want comprehensive and full third-party coverage, sir ?" I was a little taken aback and muttered more mildly, "Yes, of course."

"I'll put you straight through to someone who can help you, sir." Click, click, clickerty click ... Brrr, Brrr, Brrr. This time it was a man's voice and I started all over again. It was going to be quite a long business, I thought, and the idea was immediately confirmed. Lloyd's do not directly insure ordinary, common or garden things, let alone elephants. The matter should be referred to a firm of insurance Brokers.

"Do you know a firm of brokers who would take on such a risk ?" Long, long pause. Much rustling of papers and grunting.

"Well, you might try this one." He then gave me the name. "Of course, the chances are very remote but ... never say die !" I thanked the voice and was about to ring off when it came in again. "Excuse me, sir, but do you really mean to take an ELEPHANT over the ALPS ?"

"Yes, of course. Can you think of any finer holiday ?"

I dropped the receiver with a gesture of glee.

Having made the appropriate inquiries at the firm mentioned, I received a letter the next morning. These brokers seem frightfully industrious fellows. I read with eager anticipation.

We have pleasure to submit the following quotation which we have obtained from Lloyd's Underwriters:

Death from natural causes, illness or disease or from accident, fire and lightning or from destruction made necessary to terminate incurable suffering.

£8oo/£1,ooo on an elephant. Rate: £X per cent.

I danced for joy. Here was someone who was really willing to insure our elephant.

We eventually decided to try another brokers for as you will have noticed (I must admit I did not, to start with) the statement means that Jumbo is only covered for death. What if she were seriously ill ? The London Zoo put us on to a firm whose final coverage stood as follows :

On: 1 elephant—valued £1,500 (Signor Terni had given me this new figure).

Against all risks, including illness, injury, death, mortality, slaughter from motives of humanity and expenses incurred by any of the foregoing but not exceeding the sum insured. Free of capture and seizure but including strikes, riots and civil commotions.

I could anticipate civil commotion of considerable magnitude; in fact it was certain that there would be a good deal, but only on an amused, friendly level. The strikes were more difficult to visualise. Perhaps frontier police would down tools at the thought of having to stamp the passport of an elephant. Anything might happen and probably would. What ever it was, we would be insured against it.

Jumbo might sit on a bubble car. She might cause a startled pilot suddenly to crash-land his low-flying jet. She might even start a minor war between Alpine tribes eager to put the elephant to its proper use ... as a military tank. What would we do in this case ? It was quite simple ... we were insured against it! Third-party coverage of up to £50,000 seemed about as good a precaution as any. Yes, we really 'went to town' on that insurance. Having made sure that Jumbo was covered against practically every contingency, we promptly insured Ernesto, our mahout, so that practically not one hair of his head could be singed without Lloyd's forking up. Each member of the team was covered for up to £1,000. Then, as a final gesture, when plans had really started to materialise and world interest was aroused, we even insured against the expedition being prevented from starting 'from any cause whatsoever'.

All this took time and it was not until a few days before Jumbo was due to leave Turin by train for France that the finalised papers, stamped, signed and sealed, were sent out to Italy for Signor Terni's final check through and approval. I cannot think why nobody thought of insuring the safe arrival of the papers. I suppose we had to stop somewhere !

STAGE FOUR. Find a team

Richard and I sat down to make a list of all the jobs to be filled. It was formidable in length.

Leader, Secretary, Treasurer, Publicity Officer, Literary Expert (to go back to the original Greek at critical moments), Archaeologist, Veterinary Officer, Interpreter for French and Italian, Photographer, Quartermaster, Doctor (Synhalus), Horseman (to look after the mules), Cook, Chaplain (Bogus) and Leader of the Advanced Guard.

It is amazing how one's ideas change and mature through experience. At that stage, I had visualised our band being at least fifty strong. But problems of selecting, training and equipping these troops would have become so complex that there would not have been time for much else.

A key man, of course, would be our Veterinary Officer. In Colonel John Hickman, Senior Reader in Animal Surgery at the School of Veterinary Medicine, Cambridge University, we found the man in a million. He had had wide experience of elephants in India, had been in charge of the transport of a number of elephants and other animals from Germany to Holland immediately after the war and possesses a deep understanding of the ways of animals. What amazed me was that he actually wanted to come. Here was a real expert, surrounded by a group of inexperienced amateurs. Richard had gone to Professor Pugh, Head of the Cambridge Veterinary School, for advice. Did he know anyone who might be willing to come with us ? The Professor picked up the telephone, saying : "I wonder if Hickman would be interested ? He might have an idea anyway."

"Hullo, Hickman, do you know anyone interested in going with an elephant over the Alps in search of Hannibal ?" The reply came straight back without a moment's hesitation: "I'll go myself" He did, for he meant it; and the expedition was not only provided with an expert veterinary officer, with the mature knowledge and experience needed for such an enterprise, but also a medical officer par excellence.

At first we took a very strong line about women. "No, it would be quite impossible to have ladies on the expedition," went our constant song. Even Elizabeth, who was as full-blooded a Hannibalian as anyone, had no entry into this all-male team. Slowly and inevitably we weakened, and finally capitulated. How glad I am ! We realised that we would have to have cooks. Cooks would have to be feminine. Charming and highly competent lady cooks we would-and did-have. So it was that Clare Harden-Smith and Cynthia Pilkington joined the ranks.

There is now no doubt that they were worth their weight in gold. Clare had studied zoology at Dublin University and was due to go to America on a scholar- ship the following September for two years. I have always teased Clare about her love for horses. Having been practically brought up in the saddle, the prospect of riding an elephant over the Alps may have seemed only logical. I accordingly appointed her commander-in-chief of the cavalry. In fact, this entailed the care of the two expedition mules. They would be hired as we went along and though each would have its local driver, someone had to supervise loading and unloading, feeding times, etc. Cynthia was studying at Homerton Teachers' Training College at Cambridge. Her background of wide travel, experience on such things as TV and excellent command of languages were to prove most useful. The second job we gave her was far more formidable than cooking food. It might have entailed cooking the finances, though as far as I know she never had to resort to such extremity. As treasurer she would by no means have an easy time for not only were there francs, lire, and pounds to be juggled with, all at the same time, but also the allocation of items of expenditure and the punctual paying-off of' friendly tribes', muleteers and others.

As expedition cameraman we had Jimmy Song, a theological student who came from Singapore and whom Elizabeth introduced to the circle. He had had a wide experience of photography through working on semi-professional jobs with a leading London agency during vacations. The task we set him during the expedition was onerous, though extremely stimulating: Armed with a Leica, an Agfa

Silette and a cine camera he was expected to provide :

(i) A complete set of black and white stills for the expedition's use and the photograph albums we planned to present to the mayors of Rome, Turin, Susa and Montmelian and to send to the firms who provided us with free equipment.

(ii) A set of coloured slides for each member of the expedition and

(iii) A colour cine-film of about twenty to thirty minutes' duration.

Richard and I had both known Michael Hetherington from college days, when he had read classics, and he was now invited to become quartermaster and literary expert. Then on the last lap of a Diploma of Education course at Cambridge, he commenced teaching at Aldenham School in the following September. Till then his life would be filled with details of expedition equipment, their acquisition, their maintenance during the-journey and finally their disposal. Moreover, his classical training put the expedition on a firm academic footing. In the event of a professor's sudden appearance and challenge to our understanding of the original Greek of Polybius, Mike would be called to the rescue.

By making Richard secretary and leader of the advance guard and me, leader and publicity officer, the expedition had a full complement and, in fact, satisfied all but two of the original requirements. We did not have an archaeologist since, even though tumuli of possible interest had been sighted on the Col de Clapier it was still uncertain if their investigation would be worth while. Mrs. Brogan, who is a leading expert on Alpine digs, promised to hold herself in readiness to fly out if anything promising was found. Our Italian interpreter would be Ernesto and that brings me to possibly the most important man of all. Ernesto (or Ernst) Gobold was Jumbo's mahout and trainer, an Austrian by birth, with wide experience of elephants in Britain and the continent. At one time he had worked with Bertram Mills's circus so that his English was good. He had been with Signor Terni for some time now and was to prove himself a man of tremendous stamina, patience and courage. Also from the 'Gardino Zoologico' at Turin came the driver of the expedition food lorry-Signor Baldi. We called him Garibaldi for short and found him the most cheerful of companions. He was always happy.

The selected team was invited to a week-end at Cambridge on the 13th -14th June to get to know each other, settle organisation problems and clarify the academic question. The expedition leader and secretary presented the case for Clapier as clearly as possible and left the others to make up their own minds. After all, we were going on a quest, not simply a journey of verification and it was important that those who had not already been over the Alpine passes should postpone their final decision. Everyone had been issued with a long list of books to read, varying from Polybius, Book III, Livy, Book XXI and the Journal of Roman Studies 1956, to Seven League Boots by Richard Halliburton, describing his crossing of the Great St. Bernard Pass with an elephant in 1937. These we discussed with enthusiasm. Our aims in this respect were summarised in the third and last circular to the team:

'Technique: We must all clearly realise that smooth organisation, while vitally important, is insufficient to ensure success in presenting our message. Jumbo will sell herself. Our part is to make the background of equal interest and to get across the real question of Hannibal's route. Our technique needs thought and preparation-not to know all the answers, but to appreciate which questions matter.'

We now had our team, not only fully fitted for their individual jobs but also equipped for classical argument.

STAGE FIVE. Equip your expedition

'Ladies first', they say, so we turn to Jumbo. Besides food and loving attention, what else would she need.

The idea of elephant boots had first come from Mr. Oliver Graham-Jones, M.R.C.V.S., Curator of Mammals and Veterinary

43

Officer at the London Zoo. As a precautionary measure it seemed excellent and we immediately scouted around for a firm which might make such things.

Meanwhile, I wrote off to Signor Terni for his elephant's foot measurements. Within a week we had received a large envelope from Turin and inside lay four pieces of brown paper smelling rather of the zoo! Jumbo had clearly stood on them and had her big, flat feet traced around with a crayon. They had not been washed. I carried the priceless footprints to my room, rather secretively, I remember, for fear that someone would notice their smell and then, wrapping them carefully in white tissue paper, slipped them rather foolishly into the 'Hannibal' drawer. I fear that some of the letters sent out on expedition-crested writing- paper bore the faint scent of ' elephant'.

It was to Lotus that we eventually turned for help and Mr. Tysoe, manager of their Northampton factory, kindly consented to make us the boots. I immediately posted off the footprints, rather glad to get rid of them, and yet strangely attached to them in a sentimental way. They were the only link we had with the elephant we had never seen. Colonel Hickman had had experience of elephant boots in India so he undertook their design and made several journeys to Northampton during the next few weeks. It was indeed a development project, for never before had boots been made for this type of requirement, and step by step the Colonel and Mr. Tysoe worked out the pattern. The four boots were to be functional, not beautiful; but the results were magnificent-great, studded leather soles with the best quality waterproof leather sides for the first four inches and then canvas leggings to a height of thirty inches. Each boot was so beautifully made that the touch of the master craftsman was unmistakable. They fitted perfectly and this is all the greater compliment to the makers of the biggest boots in the world, to remember that they had nothing to work from save four scrappy bits of paper.

Jumbo's jacket was, again, of first quality. The making of the flax canvas 'jumper' became a combined operation between the Flaxspinners and Manufacturers' Association of Dundee and John Smith & Co., the well-known firm of sailmakers. It was to be waterproof and padded to withstand the cold and would need ten yards of thirty-six-inch-wide material. Once again we faced the problem of making it to size with its prospective wearer hundreds of miles away—so the zoo sent Jumbo's vital statistics, marked against

44

a rough sketch of an elephant. I discovered that Jumbo was thirteen feet, or one hundred and fifty-six inches, around the waist and wondered what kind of tape measure had been available for such an enormous dimension.

Some might argue that as Hannibal did not have jackets and boots for his elephants we should not, either. But ours was an investigation of relative performance, not of comparison through exact similarity. Moreover, the equipment was purely precautionary and would not be used unless absolutely necessary.

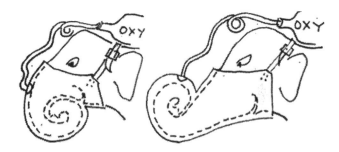

A further precaution was taken, for it had been noticed that when Jumbo climbed really steep ascents, in a trial run on Mont Supergo behind Turin, she was inclined to use her leading knee to lever herself up. The Cottenham saddlers made a pair of splendid knee-pads, looking rather like Carthaginian shields and bearing a medallion of stout brass studs, to the Colonel's design.

It would have been interesting to try out oxygen equipment on the elephant, though, of course, quite impracticable. In light-hearted vein, I wrote to Sir John Hunt. His reply, in a similar mood, is worth quoting:

"I was, of course, intrigued over the prospect of administering oxygen to your elephant! Presumably, if you propose to re-enact the journey in the manner of Hannibal, you have found evidence that his elephants were also equipped in this way. Any such information would be of great interest to our scientists. I might be able to help you over this question of oxygen apparatus for the elephant; on hearing from you, I will endeavour to make arrangements with the firm of Norma/air for a suitable mask design. It seems to me important to establish in what position the elephant's trunk will be

45

carried, before the design is made; should it be curled upwards or downwards or held straight? He will undoubtedly need training and probably a decompression-chamber test. The construction of a special chamber for this purpose will be an expensive item.

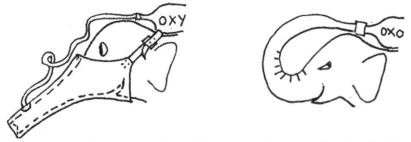

Finally, there is the question of warm clothing to fit the elephant. Dark goggles would be essential and I agree he may need footwear on snow, and perhaps some specially constructed crampons. I shall be most interested to hear from you again. Yours, etc."

It struck me later that the trunk could be used as the pipe linking oxygen cylinders, obviously strapped to the back, and lungs. What more efficient apparatus could one have ! If only the men climbing Everest had had trunks the mountain would have been conquered years ago.

In comparison with these fascinating and highly original pieces of equipment, that for the remaining members of the expedition seems quite mundane; four tents, sleeping-bags, two primus stoves, a guitar, cooking equipment, Grenfell jackets (supplied free of charge) and so on. There was, however, one piece of equipment which we had to share with Jumbo, for she liked it so much. It was the expedition mouth organ!

STAGE SIX. Get the elephant fighting fit! (Hannibal's must have been)

With the odour of elephant emanating from that 'Hannibal' drawer, it was little wonder that Richard and I wanted to meet Jumbo herself and see her capabilities before we went much further. Easter was chosen for the reconnaissance patrol and we decided to motor down to Turin. It would give an opportunity to contact the mayors of the towns along our route. Signor Terni welcomed us cordially and together we walked over to the elephant house. This was quite a grand affair with its own swimming pool and fancy railing. We shook hands with Ernesto who then led us indoors to meet Jumbo. He armed us with apples for there was no better way of making friends with his charge than to toss a few down her throat. Here she stood, swaying slightly from side to side and eyeing us with interest; a fine young lady, over eight feet high. We soon made friends. That afternoon, we made an appointment with her on Mont Supergo to put her through her paces. She proved very fit and healthy but would have to gain more confidence on steep gradients. Ernesto had already been taking her out on training runs and now that he had a better idea of the kind of gradient she would be tackling in the Alps, these outings would be intensified and made more rigorous. There is no doubt he did an excellent job of this by the time of the big trek, for not only were Jumbo's feet in tough walking condition as a result of her constant exercise but her agility and stamina would have matched many a Carthaginian elephant.

STAGE SEVEN. Find the necessary money

As you will appreciate, this was going to be no cheap expedition. Insurance alone amounted to a considerable sum. Then there would be the elephant's transport from Turin to the starting point, food, equipment, hire of pack-mules and so on. How were we to come by so much money? The answer lay in the world interest immediately evident on the news of the proposed journey being sent out over Reuter in February. Until then everything had been kept strictly secret as several important arrangements were not finalised. The leak came through Italy and immediately Pressmen from the continent and Britain traced me from my home at Reigate, to the Y.M.C.A. at Birmingham, to the office where I normally work, and finally to the branch factory where a friend and I happened to be that afternoon, writing a report on a recent business visit to Germany. All afternoon the telephone rang and trunk calls came in from London, Copenhagen and Paris. No wonder the report was left unfinished.

One thing was evident. The world was interested. Could we not channel this world interest to assist us financially ? So it was that we moved towards a contract of co-operation, for news before and during the journey, with some newspaper. The expedition had been born in a world of academic reasoning. Since then outstanding personages had been contacted, for advice or assistance, or had written direct to us. In my file I have an interesting collection of correspondence, amongst which are letters from Her Serene Highness Princess Grace of Monaco, Mrs. Chamberlain, His Royal Highness the Duke of Edinburgh, Lord Montgomery, Sir John Hunt, Sir James Wordie, Sir Mortimer Wheeler, Senator Sibille of Rome, Dr. Lavis-Trafford, Dr. Lang of Basle, Dr. Julian de Zulueta, Danny Kaye and Stirling Moss. We did not want to sell our 'academic integrity for money', especially with a man of the calibre of Doctor McDonald as Expedition President, and yet, clearly the appeal of an elephant going over the Alps was universal and the story was worthy of presentation to as wide a public as possible.

The Daily Mail seemed an obvious first choice for, only a year earlier, it had bought the exclusive news right in the 'Small World' balloon expedition. Its wide readership, excellent presentation and reliability in not submerging the academic side of the subject in eagerness to present 'human interest' made them outstanding claimants. On the very evening of the Reuter report, the paper had sent a member of its headquarters staff from London to Birmingham to express interest in the news rights. But somehow, intangibly, things were not materialising. It was not until 3rd June that we learnt that the paper would be unable to link up with us and why. The problem was that the Bleriot Memorial Air Race from Marble Arch to the Arc de Triomphe, which the paper was sponsoring, overlapped our journey by several days. The Mail would have had too much on its plate. Confused readers might imagine Jumbo arriving out of breath at the Arc de Triomphe to be told by a gendarme that she should be beating Hannibal over the Alps, not trying to compete against the Army, Navy and Air Force! We fully understood and dropped the matter.

It was at the most critical stage of the printing strike. Daily newspapers were being threatened with stoppage and there is little wonder that great concern filled expedition members. Nevertheless, we courageously walked one block down Bouverie Street, showed our cards at the door of the News Chronicle and within ten days had a contract in our hands. We liked the Chronicle's approach and looked forward to close-co-operation on the journey. We hoped that its staff would like us. Financially, the complete situation was reversed. What with the money coming in from this source and from Life magazine with which we also made an agreement for North American picture rights, it looked as though there might be a little money left over and we decided to help the Wodd Refugee Year with this. At least, we hoped there would be some left over, for, as you will see from the telegram, the Life offer was scaled to the success of the expedition.

LIFE MAGAZINE OFFERS SCALED TWO HUNDRED FIFTY POUNDS FOR NORTH AMERICAN RIGHTS TO THE HANNIBAL EXPEDITION COMMA ONE HUNDRED POUNDS IF ELEPHANT GETS AWAY FROM STARTING LINE AND WALKS FOR ONE FULL DAY COMMA ONE HUNDRED ADDITIONAL POUNDS IF ELEPHANT GETS HIGH ENOUGH TO ASSURE US PICTURES WITH ALPINE BACKGROUNDS COMMA FIFTY ADDITIONAL POUNDS IF ELEPHANT COMPLETES JOURNEY TO TURIN STOP SINCE THERE IS ACTUALLY VERY LITTLE WHICH CAN BE KEPT FROM OTHER PHOTOGRAPHERS LIFE WOULD LIKE TO HAVE ELEPHANT SHOE PIXS AND SHOTS FROM BACK OF ELEPHANT EXCLUSIVELY AND ALSO MINIMAL MATERIAL FOR SHORT TEXT BLOCK WHICH WOULD NOT BE DETAILED BUT WOULD SAY WHAT THE EXPEDITION HOPES TO PROVE COMMA HOW THEY WENT ABOUT IT AND WHETHER THEY DID INDEED PROVE ANYTHING STOP THIS SHORT AMOUNT OF WRITTEN MATERIAL WOULD NOT I'M SURE INTERFERE WITH YOUR SUBSEQUENT DETAILED STORY STOP

So here we were—the 'British Alpine Hannibal Expedition' with an elephant who was fighting fit, a route, insurance, a team, equipment (including elephant boots and jacket) and the necessary money. Only stage eight lay ahead. That was: to take the elephant over the Alps.

To see this operation in full perspective, it is worth noting the aims of the expedition:

(1) Historical Investigation

(i) To make an itinerary study of the crucial nine days of Hannibal's route, on a day-by-day basis and verify a theory placing those nine days between Pontcharra and the Col de Clapier.

(ii) To make a complete photographic record of this stretch, indicating important landmarks and the exact views that Hannibal would have seen.

(iii) To survey possible archaeological sites for future investigation.

(2) Popular History

To so interest the public through the journey that they might catch something of the fascination of history and be all the more ready to study and learn from it.

(3) International Friendship

To go, as it were, as ambassadors of peace and strengthen the ties between our country, France and Italy through spontaneous enthusiasm for a common cause-the quest for Hannibal, and the delightful personality of an elephant.

(4) Refugees

To channel public interest to constructive good by donating all proceeds of the expedition, above the running costs, to the W odd Refugee Year, for children's work.

(5) Challenge

To meet the personal challenge to self-discipline and careful, thorough thinking and action presented to each of us on the team and also to satisfy that intangible Joie de vivre and love for adventure that is in us all, the world over.

PART TWO
THE JOURNEY

CHAPTER VII

Send-off from Montmélian

STEAM HISSED OUT from under the bonnet and a heavy Humber Snipe came to a halt beside the straight French road. It was very dark and two figures groaned, switched on a torch and climbed wearily out. They were Richard and Michael. This was the third time the fine veteran had boiled over and the two leant over the bonnet with great concern. Somehow or other, they, and all the equipment, would have to arrive at Montmélian early next day. A moment's glance at the back seats, buckling roof rack and luggage carrier would persuade one that a hundred and five pieces of equipment could not easily be moved on to another vehicle. How- ever, impossible as the task seemed, there was no alternative and certainly not a moment to lose. The car would have to be left in the keeping of a local garage.

After much trouble, a telephone was reached, a morose garage proprietor contacted and every article of equipment unpacked and transferred to a lorry. This raced to the nearest station, a good fifty kilometres away, at a phenomenal speed in order to catch the night express to Montmélian. Every one of the hundred and five bits and pieces had to be labelled, so that two team members, now completely exhausted and expecting the train to arrive at any moment, settled down to frantically scribbling 'Hannibal, Montmélian' on fortunately available labels. I would not be at all surprised if the station ran out of labels on that occasion. Porters and guards stood encircling the two kneeling figures and their mammoth pile under the gas light and seemed highly amused; they laughed and joked but not one would stir a finger to help. This seemed cruel. However, from the way the two recounted their adventures to me later, it appears they endured with stoic fortitude. After all, we might say, Hannibal did not really get much help from the Gallic tribes through whose territory he had passed.

So it was that, having woken from uneasy sleep on a night express couchette, grabbed a towel and, half awake, staggered down the corridor to have a wash, I saw Richard's tired face looking at me from its other end. I blinked my eyes and started to fight my way towards him, through the crowd which packed the corridor, propping itself up on suitcases and in various stages of sleep. When we met, the story was told and we sat down to work out the awesome implications of having no car.

Montmélian is a small but prosperous wine manufacturing town, set in the wide Isere valley. It nestles at the foot of a cliff—surrounded hill which commands the valley's full breadth and, therefore, is of immense strategic importance. No wonder the ruins of a might fortress are to be found there. In medieval times, Montmélian had been the capital of Savoie and ruled over vast areas of the Alps, its sway reaching over the present frontiers to the Piedmont Plains in Italy. A more suitable place for starting the expedition would be difficult to find. It was within a few hours' easy march from Hannibal's 'Ascent towards the Alps' at Pontcharra, and its fortress, on the very stones of which we were to start our journey, had in bygone days commanded not only Col Clapier but the very ground of our final destination, the Zoological Gardens at Turin. The views from the fortress were superb and on a clear day one could even see the mighty massif of Mont Blanc over to the north-east. Finally, the friendship, hospitality and wholehearted backing of the Mayor, Monsieur Serraz and his friends gave us a wonderful send-off.

The train drew up with a jolt. The team, which was already on its toes and ready for almost anything after such an unpredicted start, scrambled down the steps (for as with most French stations there was no platform) and dashed to the luggage wagon to unload the hundred and five articles. What a curious mixture- packets of cake, cartons of tinned food, Tilly lamps, tents, rope, an elephant's knee-pad, a box of 'smarter' clothes, and so on. All this paraphernalia was loaded on to a rickety old station wagon ... a vast mountain, crowned majestically with an elephant boot ! Everybody had to help to hold things steady, for the path across the lines to smoother ground was far from even, the cart had no sides and before we had moved even two yards, three things had fallen off.

A far more genteel 'unloading' was to take place that afternoon, pictures of which were flashed across the world, to be seen on television screens as far away as San Francisco. The owner of the boot was waiting quietly in her railway compartment on a siding. Her train journey from Turin had gone well. American papers insist that the wagon was labelled 'Fragile'. I had not noticed it but welcomed some railway official's good humour. All that could be seen was a long, inquisitive nose, protruding from the pitch darkness of the entrance into the bright sunlight, rapacious, eager to feel all, smell all, and, if possible, grab all that was edible to feed that huge mass of elephant. Zero hour for the grand unloading was drawing near. Crowds started to gather, and the team, together with the Mayor, the British Vice-Consul from Lyons, the Italian Consul, wives, interpreters and a whole host of press-men, gathered near the waving trunk. There was a hold-up. The band had not arrived. Then they arrived, roaring down upon us in a huge charabanc, and out they tumbled, dressed in black pork- pie hats and off-white, homespun jackets. As the V.I.P.s stood in a semi-circle around the open wagon door, the band played the National Anthems of Italy, France and Britain, and then marched over to take its place in the long procession which was being formed. Jumbo stepped out of the wagon and took her place. The Mayor raised his hand, and at the signal we were off.

First came the fire brigade with their chromium-plated helmets specially polished for the occasion. They sat high in their two red chariots of peace. Behind them marched the band, sixty strong, and by this time really warmed up, and in their wake, the dancers, ladies in beautifully embroidered shawls and men in silk waist- coats. The Queen of the show, Jumbo herself, waved her trunk to the music and plodded forward with steady deliberation. Then came the team, accompanied by the Mayor, Consuls and others, and close behind the three mules with their drivers. Their job would be to carry our equipment during the daily march and to look picturesque.

Last, but not least, in quantity as well as in importance, followed, pushed, jostled, shouted, sang the general populace, all in a fever of excitement and delight. There was a halt. Evidently, the fire brigade had taken the wrong turning. General chaos ensued but, as if by magic, the long procession quickly put itself in order and set off again, this time in the right direction. With the safe arrival of everyone at the Fort, the afternoon's fiesta commenced. There was no lack of variety here. The dancers skipped in animated circles around Jumbo, posing in a myriad of positions for the photographers. The choir, who also had come to the hilltop, stilled the multitude and sang old folk lullabys, the band interposing with odd medleys. Everybody enjoyed them- selves enormously; while Jumbo stood a little apart, scratching her back on a tree, eyeing the whole proceedings with what I took to be amused interest.

I walked along with the Mayor, both of us exclaiming with delight every now and then. He spoke hardly any English and my French is weak so the same words had to be used over and over again. 'Tres Joli. Formidable. Merveilleux'. This wonderful party was all his doing and the genius of his imagination. What finer send-off could we have than a fiesta where local talent was shown to its fullest ? Moreover, he was fertile in ideas for raising money to cover costs for the day's proceedings and had had special medal- lions made to commemorate the occasion. These were selling 'like hot cakes', at two hundred francs each (three shillings) and if anyone, young or old, was not wearing a 'Hannibal Caravan' badge the Mayor's youthful assistants would pounce upon him and make him buy of their wares.

The Chief of the County Police was there also, in an immaculate uniform, and with him his entire family. To see the exalted figure join in with the local police in gaily trying to stop people pressing too closely around Jumbo, gives some indication of the exuberant atmosphere.

At last, the shadows lengthened, the vins d' honneur had been drunk and, as the crowds dispersed one was able to see the grass on the castle grounds instead of just one solid mass of people. The British Consul and I rode down into the town on the back of a fire wagon, each wearing a fire helmet and feeling, in truth, members of the community. Jumbo lumbered back to her wagon to take a good night's sleep in preparation for the next day's march. The rest of us returned to our hotel, had an hour's quiet rest and then resumed the foray at a 'Grand Reception' banquet given in the honour of 'Elephant and Expedition'. Here we all were, a wide variety of people, of every status and temperament, brought together in friendliness by a pachyderm. A bearded muleteer sat joking with a press photographer.

The wife of an English correspondent discussed politics with the Mayor of a town farther up the valley. With wild gesticulations, the Town Clerk excitedly explained an old French fable to the expedition cook. It was not until well after midnight that the call for 'musica' slowly hushed the conversation. Our three sturdy muleteers, each with a magnificent black beard, stepped out, produced great, winding horns, and turned with their backs to the assembled company so that the bell of each instrument pointed directly at us. The ensuing music was distinctly bacchantine and had such force to it that one was almost thrown backwards; a delightful way to end an evening. No one had any reason to be dozing at such a party but if they had been a little on the sleepy side, now they would walk home quite wide awake!

Next day, the expedition started in earnest, but pomp and ceremony were by no means ended. The homespun band returned to see Jumbo off and marched along with us from the top of the fort. Here the Mayor kindly cut a bright red ribbon, thoughtful gift from my sister, and so made a ceremonial of Jumbo's path to glory. At the boundary of the town, which is marked by a garage, it was clearly time for a final vin d'honneur, a last salvo of marching tunes from the band, and the long road ahead. However, as was confirmed daily, our elephant and water had a strange affinity for each other and she more or less insisted that the garage hose-pipe should be turned on her. She was obviously delighted and with that strange ironical humour elephants have, squirted water all over the filling-station attendant; fine thanks to the last inhabitant of Montmélian for a send off even the most forgetful of pachyderms would never forget.

CHAPTER VIII

First Day's March

POLYBIUS WRITES :

'After a ten-day march along the bank of the Skaras (Isere) Hannibal began his ascent of the Alps. Allobrogians from a prosperous town ahead planned an ambuscade but this was fortunately discovered. After approaching the dangerous point on the first day of the "Ascent" Hannibal captured the enemy position that night and on the second day, took the Allobrogian town. He had suffered heavy casualties.'

[Note: We place the start to the Ascent at Pontcharra, the point of ambuscade in the gorge above the town and the enemy town at La Rochette.]

The sun beat down, the drone of flies hung heavily on the air and we plodded along a dusty road. Glamour there had been but now remained the plain down-to-earth fact that we had to walk with an elephant over the Alps. Simple as this might seem some of its implications were foreboding. I was very conscious of the pressures beginning to bear upon me, the surrounding press of reporters and photographers, the needs of the team, the necessity for good lines of communication and, by no means least, the demands of Jumbo. I considered that it would only be possible to fully cope with these pressures, so long as I could stay fresh men- tally and physically and maintain a one-move-ahead position in the day-to-day plan. This plan had been prepared months before. Specially printed sheets, distributed to the team, close friends and allied Press, stated the distances to be travelled each day, and the positions for camping, and held a table, equating these to Polybius' description of Hannibal's march.

Communications were vitally important and extremely difficult to maintain at a high level of efficiency. This matter not only involved information passed within the team and to and from Jumbo, via Ernesto, but also contact with the Press, who so easily misunderstood actions or tended to twist them to their own ends. As Ernesto was able to speak English and Italian he also became our chief contact with Baldi, who as driver of the expedition lorry was custodian of elephant food. As he spoke not a word of English nor we Italian, Ernesto was rather important.

One of our main tasks was to keep to Polybius' schedule and meanwhile to study the elephant's behaviour and speeds at varying altitudes and conditions. To do this an altimeter and pedometer were used to obtain readings which, taken every half-hour, were entered in the expedition log-book, to give a detailed story of the journey.

At Pontcharra we commenced the real journey 'in Hannibal's tracks' ; rather like Good King Wenceslas' page, we began to place our footsteps in those of the great army, on a day-by-day stride basis. Till then, it had been a matter of getting into position, but now, out came all our instruments and a strict record of the elephant's progress was made.

While Richard and the Colonel went ahead to have a close look at the Col de Clapier, the rest of the team, together with Jumbo, the three mules, their drivers, a whole host of children and a van from the local newspaper loudly broadcasting 'hit' music as it went, passed on through Pontcharra up towards the 'ascent'. No wonder French locals dubbed our expedition' Hannibal Caravan' ! The town itself was full to overflowing with local people, peasants from the surrounding area, shopkeepers galore, for they flourish in France, holiday—makers and housewives. Funnily enough there were practically no pressmen ! Where was the hustling, bustling crowd of photographers and reporters who had thronged around us at Montmélian? Indeed, the number had reached astonishing proportions. At least nine nations had been represented—television, radio, magazines, newsreels, picture agencies and daily Press. They had all been out in force.

Now, however, at Pontcharra, the Press was most conspicuous by its absence. The truth was revealed to me later by one of its number. The Mayor of La Rochette, our planned resting place for the night, had inveigled the Press to a general party with iced drinks and swimming-pool laid on, and all at his expense. With his warm invitation came the remark: "Don't bother to wait for the caravan at Pontcharra. The elephant is not going there anyway." Resulting from this, very few reports or pictures of Jumbo passing through Pontcharra were ever published. The motive for the Mayor's cunning action, friendly rivalry between the two towns !

We passed on under a gruelling sun, in high spirits and without mishap. The gorge narrowed until it was barely wide enough for the road and single track railway to push their way through. Surely it was in such surroundings that Hannibal had had his first really difficult piece of country. There is no doubt that La Rochette had been a most strategic town during bygone ages and it might well have been so in 218 B.C. ! Hannibal could easily have made this short cut through the gorge, rather than follow round the easier and more recognised route along the Isere-Arc valleys, due to his need of supplies, after ten days' march from the Island. La Rochette would have been no meagre town to capture. I stopped continually and made a series of sketches of the changing profile of the gorge walls. Jumbo just kept plodding on. Her speed was steady and but for the flies, she was obviously enjoying the whole thing. The pedometer did not indicate as accurately as we might have hoped but gave consistent readings. To obtain a completely true picture of Jumbo distances covered, an 'elephant-size' pedometer attached to her leg, would have been necessary. However, as the 'market for these would, no doubt, be extremely limited and the chances of it being broken during the first half- mile good, we used a man-sized instrument which was adjusted to the average pace. It was the best we could do in the circumstances.

If, as we believe, Hannibal had taken the ancient La Rochette by surprise (while many of its inhabitants were out fighting his men in the gorge), there is little doubt that we did not take it unawares. One man assured me that never had so many people assembled there. I added "Since Hannibal's 50,000 strong force had done so," and we laughed. Some had waited hours. Some had walked almost as far as Jumbo. The market stood packed with people, children very much to the fore. A kind of Western cowboy corral surrounded the square and this was hung thick with urchins, like a swarm of bees on a stick.

There in the centre stood two long tables, graced by dazzling white cloths and the local wine, Sourire de Savoie. Everyone was so excited, so talkative, so pleased that we had come, so glad that old Madame Dufey (or whatever her name might have been) had also come to see the elephant. What could be finer than a large, lovable animal convening a reunion.

By the time the expedition reached Turin we had heard an incredible variety of bands. This particular one played with great gusto. It was much smaller than the Montmélian band, more personal and wore uniforms and everyday working clothes all mixed together. I would not have been surprised if most of the players did not work in the Formica factory, the only local industry, which finishes work at 6.o p.m., the time that we arrived, and dashed out to welcome us.

After the National Anthems and vin d'honneur, a large fat man led forward the tiniest of donkeys, called Albert, pulling a bright yellow cart piled high with vegetables and fruit. Albert did no like Jumbo, nor Jumbo Albert, but the length of a trunk and a cart separated them so Jumbo ate her fill ! We walked wearily to the camp site. This had been carefully prepared by Michael and Garibaldi. The setting was ideal, an open field beside a barn with water near at hand. With elephant tethered to a sufficiently stout tree, eating a good meal (Albert's cart-load might be considered a mere cart-load of hors d'oeuvres), we busily made ready for the evening's reception and dinner.

The Colonel and Richard arrived at about 10.0 p.m., tired and extremely hungry. They had been without food for hours and had had an extremely wearying time. It was not that the ascent to the Col de Clapier had given any difficulty. No, the going had been quite all right and, they reported, with care it would be passable for Jumbo. The trouble began on the return journey when, having reached Montmélian through lifts along the main road, they tried to get some means of transport to La Rochette. Our friends of yesterday, the shouting animated crowd, turned a deaf ear to their entreaties and no one would help them-not even 'for Jumbo's sake'. Such is the irony of world fame. A mahout is not without honour, save in the country from whence he has led his elephant!

The team left dinner early. It was a drastic measure to be taken by a leader who did not often ignore the yearnings of his stomach, but it was better to do this than finally get to bed at 1.0 a.m. as on the previous night. This was one of our biggest problems, that of not getting overtired, without being discourteous to our many and generous hosts. "It is not easy for ordinary people to be plunged into the intense limelight of world interest," we would quietly murmur to each other in moments of complete exhaustion. Jumbo could not have been ordinary for she took it in her stride !

A five-foot deep mattress of hay seemed preferable to the hard ground so I moved my sleeping-bag over to the large wall-less barn near the camp and in the moonlight scribbled closing notes to the day's log readings. Only fifteen yards away, loomed the huge form of our elephant. The moonlight shone through dancing leaves, stirred by the evening wind and played weird patterns on her broad, bristled back. I wondered if this whole journey was not just some fantastic dream and turned over in my sleeping-bag. We had marched the first day's itinerary and all was well!

CHAPTER IX

Second Day's March

(Hannibal's Fourth from the Beginning of the 'Ascent')

POLYBIUS WRITES:

'In the enemy town Hannibal had just captured, there was a supply of corn and cattle enough for three days provision and he rested there for one whole day. (This would be Hannibal's third from the beginning of the Ascent.) On the fourth day Hannibal resumed his march and was unhindered for the next three.'

[Note: This implies that Hannibal was able to cover considerable distance during those three days and from a study of the speed of an army of Hannibal's size, with elephants, in mountain terrain we can assume an average of thirteen to fifteen miles a day. This is the speed we maintained for our next three days.]

By the next day, Tuesday, 21st July, we were able to settle into some sort of routine, as far as this is possible on an elephant journey. After general reveille had been sounded everyone would get their own personal belongings packed. Meanwhile, Cynthia or Clare lit the primus and Ernesto fed Jumbo. Breakfast would then follow and during it I would run over the plans for the day and split the team into two; the main party and a reconnaissance patrol. Richard, permanent leader of the latter, would forge ahead in the lorry with another member of the team and Baldi. Their job was to find the Mayor of the next town, get a suitable camping site, buy provisions, prepare for the main party's arrival and then rejoin us, leaving someone on guard at the camp. After breakfast every- one would break camp, the Quartermaster and cooks dealing with stores while the rest of us folded tents and loaded the equipment on to the lorry.

Eight o'clock was the scheduled time for starting so that a good portion of the day's march could be covered before the heat of midday set in. On this particular day we were not off until eight-thirty. The reason: Jumbo's eye. Flies had been a particular nuisance the previous day and one of these had bitten her beneath the lower eyelid. Colonel Hickman took out the expedition first-aid equipment in its beautifully prepared army ammunition box (sky blue with bright red crosses on each side). The eye was dressed with suitable ointment while the rest of the team either stood around watching or amused themselves by reading reports of the previous day's march in the national and local Press. Slowly, we became used to the fact that our elephant's passage was 'news' in a big way, though not until the end did we realise that as far away as New Zealand and South America the journey was being followed in every detail.

By this time the Press had started to arrive and, indeed, here was another routine. Day by day, the Press appeared and proved an endless source of interest to the expedition, which was some slight return for their interest in us. They could be divided into two groups, 'regulars' who were prepared to stick with us through thick and thin, from start to finish and the 'irregulars', those who might tag on for a day or two and then vanish for a while. Thor Heyerdahl, leader of the Kon Tiki Expedition, describes the life of ocean sharks; how each would have a number of small pilot fish precede it in close formation. It is nonsense to compare Jumbo to a shark (for they could not be more unlike in nature), but there is little doubt that we humans clustered in shoals rather like pilot fish. The 'irregular fish' would follow gleefully for a while and then dart off to some other item of news and others would come in their place.

Chief among the 'regulars' was the News Chronicle contingent. This was reasonable enough as the expedition had an agreement to co-operate with the Chronicle and give their reporters some exclusive contes. Not that the incidents surrounding an elephant trundling over the Alps can possibly be kept exclusive but there was clearly, behind every incident, an 'inside' story and the Chronicle were to have it. Life magazine had photographic rights for North America so its two representatives, Timothy Green and David Lees, were in the same category and could certainly be considered as 'regulars'. While in France, the newspaper Dauphine Libere which is distributed widely over the Alpine districts, followed us carefully and not only described journey incidents but also had a long article on the problem of Hannibal's route. It was most pleasing to discover that the occasional paper was prepared to go deeper than an account of the novelty of an elephant crossing the Alps.

Charlie Hampsher, the Daily Express reporter, would have been the most persistent 'regular' of them all had not Head Office recalled him after only three days. He had resolutely bought a sky-blue racing bicycle and planned to do his Hannibal on wheels: fine optimism to choose a racer. So attached did he become to the expedition that really our group never felt quite complete without its cycle companion after he had left. We will never forget his patient figure, bent forward over those extra- ordinary racing handle-bars, wearing a thick tweed jacket, his balding head exposed to the scorching sun. The terribly hot weather seemed no hindrance to his enjoyment of the journey. (I was reminded of Ralph Izzard of the Daily Mail arriving at one of the camps on the Everest Expedition in gym shoes.

Inappropriateness of dress is one of the first ploys of gamesmanship!)

As I was saying, the Press arrived. Here came the cream Consul with the News Chronicle team intact. Stephen Barber, Assistant Editor and Correspondent, his wife who acted as chauffeur and chief supplier of suntan ointment for the team, and John Silverside, the Chronicle photographer, were all there. John has a magnificent beard, easily discernible in the periodic whirl of cameras, a beard outpassing by a long chalk the short, stubby one of the Daily Express cameraman. It was nice to be surrounded by beards, one felt nearer to the times of Hannibal!

Life magazine were first on the scene that second day and were already taking several photographs of the camp, Jumbo's eye and of the odd elephant boot lying around. A French photographer with rimless glasses also poked about. Timothy Green, 'Life man', rather indignantly pointed him out, in the act of taking a picture of the boot. This was the kind of emergency I, as leader, had to face and found it best to be on the safe side. We all ejected' Mr. Rimless' and I promised Tim that he and John Silverside could have a private viewing of Jumbo trying on her boots early next morning when no one else was around. The boot was obviously considered an exclusive shot, whether off or on.

At last we set out, with all-important accoutrements at hand, the map, pedometer, altimeter, log-book and pencil, hats and sun-glasses. The narrow track from the farm swung out into what in England would be considered a 'B' road, and we set off at a steady three miles an hour. The elephant seemed quite happy at this speed and walked either on the grass verge or on the loose sand at the road's edge. She would rhythmically swing her heavy limbs and repudiate the flies with vehement blasts from her trunk. Another technique which she used was to run her trunk along the edge of the road, sucking up the dust and gravel as she walked. Throwing her trunk over her head, she blew it out and all over her back, then tossed her head forward with obvious satisfaction. This picking-up technique is reminiscent of a railway express drawing up water from a trough, set between the rails, at speed. The uses of that trunk were innumerable.

Chamoux will not forget our visit. By the time of the party's arrival, our elephant was thirsty. Having had a good drink at the ancient fountain, she quietly wrapped her trunk around its stem and with apparent ease bent it out of true. Whether the people of Chamoux have decided to straighten it again or leave it crooked in memory of a playful pachyderm, is not known. Next time you go through Chamoux, have a look.

Deep in a gorge of the river Arc, lies the small town of Aiguebelle. It consists of one broad street, flanked by two rows of houses. Behind them rise the steep walls of the gorge. Not much of a place, and yet the reception we received there was worthy of a population ten times as large. A band awaited our arrival and we fell in behind it to march right up through the town to a lake for the vin d'honneur. Rows of small schoolboys in green shirts, obviously on holiday, lined the route and looked on the extraordinary procession with open mouths. They, in turn, were surveyed by a number of young monks who seemed very much in control and showed delight that, as one told me, their school children would now have something to write home about.

On Jumbo's arrival at the lake, hosemen of the town's fire service gave her a thorough wash down and in the process, somehow managed to soak a large proportion of the populace. Broad smiles on the faces of the fire- men enhanced the scene of havoc. The children's paper hats were sodden and drooping, the photographers were carefully wiping the spotted lenses of their cameras and the crowd were wringing out their clothes when at last the water was turned off. Everyone laughed and soon forgot their plight in watching a large bouquet of deep red, salmon pink and white gladioli, which had been presented to the expedition by the Mayor's five-year-old daughter, being rescued from Jumbo. Contrary to the general rule this lady did not seem particularly adept in handling a bouquet and she seemed, moreover, unable to distinguish between gladioli and carrots.

After a very pleasant vin d' honneur in the shade of the trees by the lake, we settled down into camp not far away and prepared for another of those magnificent dinners which only the French can serve, in honour of the unusual.

CHAPTER X

Third Day's March

(Hannibal's Fifth from the Beginning of the 'Ascent')

AT FIVE O'CLOCK next morning the whine of a car's engine woke me from shallow sleep. It was Tim and David of Life magazine coming for early morning photographs. As a steel-grey dawn crept over the mountains, Jumbo posed beside the expedition lorry with a large placard-'British Alpine Hannibal Expedition' nailed to its side. One of the tents stood starkly in the foreground against the voluptuous elephant curves which were lit up by car headlamps. This photograph turned out magnificently and was later to be frontispiece of the seven-page feature presentation by Life. At the time, all I thought of was of going back to bed! How ever, dawn had come and we were soon trying on one of Jumbo's boots. Long before other pressmen had arrived, John Silverside and David Lees had enough photographs of this interesting exercise to keep the Chronicle and Life busy for a considerable time. To our delight the boots fitted beautifully. The initial problem of getting them on was overcome by slitting a leather binding near her heel, undoing all five yards of lace and placing her foot down into its depths.

To lace her up took a good quarter of an hour and much patience on the part of boot-wearer and lacer. Up the back of the boot ran twenty-five lace holes and each of these had to be threaded with the strong nylon cord. (Whenever a team member goes into a shop to buy a pair of shoes and notes how dexterously the shop girl fits the shoe on to a waiting foot, it is not surprising if he remembers the difficulties of Jumbo's fitting.) No boots were ever made with such care and thoroughness and they were completely waterproof for the lower four inches. Their wearer would never get wet feet ! Having .at last managed the boots, the knee-pads and jacket were also tried on and found to fit well. Of the equipment we had brought, the jacket proved most useful, for on cold nights in the mountains it gave the elephant added warmth and a waterproofing which could withstand any amount of rain.

Having joined the Arc at Aiguebelle, we were to travel up its course for the next four days. Wherever possible, the main Route

Nationale was avoided and we followed higher mountain paths. This not only kept our elephant on roads of about the same gradients as Hannibal, but also prevented traffic congestion and, on the law of averages, meant that the distances we covered were about the same as those of the Carthaginian army. After a level-crossing there was a long pull up from Aiguebelle to St. George, a beautiful little village, perched above the deep valley of the Arc, its old stone roofs nestling together and jutting out from the primitive farm houses in wide, generous eaves. The road levelled as we passed through pinewoods and then started to descend gently. From these first steep ascents and descents, we found that Jumbo was an excellent climber, progressing slowly but steadily. At a gradient of one in six, she would average about two and a half miles an hour without coaxing. Her speed of descent was quite phenomenal, for with slopes of gradient one in five and less, she was able to move with incredible speed, her long limbs swinging freely at the shoulder and hip and propelling that huge, voluminous body without any difficulty. Anything steeper than one in five would be traversed more cautiously, her trunk feeling the way ahead.

After three hours on the move, we came to a pattern of quiet lakes by the side of the road. I shouted over to Ernesto, suggesting that Jumbo might like to take to water. Elephants have extremely sensitive skins and if they are either induced into cold water or drink cold water immediately after a hot spell of travelling, they can catch quite a nasty cold. The temperature under Jumbo's arm-pit was always a good guide as to her condition. Such hints were learnt from Ernesto as we went along. [Indeed, there are so many fascinating things to learn about the elephant that at times, once Ernesto and the Colonel started to talk on pachydermic matters, one might have mistaken the expedition for a practical outdoor lesson in zoology.]

70

Jumbo took to the water like a duck and in this case the conditions were ideal. Down, down she went until all that could be seen was the top half of her massive head, with ears paddling gently and a trunk coming up from under the water like some Loch Ness monster. It made a superb scene, the morning breeze rippling over the calm waters and bringing over to us the heavy, contented breathing of our elephant and the wild mountain walls rising up for thousands of feet along the length of the valley. We stood watching her. I cupped my hand and shouted over to Ernesto, remarking how ironical it was that now when at last a really good photograph could have been taken, not one pressman or even a camera was in sight.

At that moment, the fast Aronde sports car of the two *Paris-Match* photographers turned the corner and bore down upon us. Out came cameras and click, click, click, our private viewing of the bathing beauty became public. The two boys from Paris were the most regular of all the Press who dogged our footsteps. Their sports car would dare the impossible in order to follow us up some rough little track. At all hours of the day and night, they would appear and be ready for the unusual photograph. It is amazing that they had not, by some uncanny instinct, managed to be there for our early morning boot session. With boundless energy, constant imagination and what seemed to us an unlimited supply of film, their record of the trip must have been superb. It was all the more disappointing to see the following week's Paris-Match magazine present some rather uninspiring photographs of Jumbo's back view. I took them over to show the lady in question. She did not seem very flattered.

After lunch in a grove of silver-birch trees, down by the fast-flowing Arc river I left the others at siesta while the local police car which had been with us for some time took me back to Epierre. At two o'clock in the afternoon nothing moves in France. The post office was naturally closed but with two smart policemen flanking me, it did not take long to arouse someone and send off my telegram. This was a daily procedure but as the message normally contained only a few words it was not very expensive. All well here. Have reached Epierre. Jumbo doing fine. Only bother are flies' was sufficient to assure Signor Terni that his elephant still progressed on schedule towards Turin.

Cynthia had gone ahead with Richard and Baldi to prepare our next camp, and the three arrived at the town hall of La Chambre at about eleven o'clock. Here was our next stopping place, a town rather larger than Aiguebelle but very much more scattered. They explored the dilapidated town hall but could find no one. The door to the room labelled 'Kindergarten' was locked; upstairs, the office, secretariat and courtroom were all visited in turn but found deserted. This town was obviously not expecting us. On the other side of the street stood a chemist's shop and it was here that things looked more hopeful. The apothecary told them that not only the Mayor but the Deputy Mayor were on holiday. However, as he happened to be the Mayor's representative, could he help them ? "We are from the British Alpine Hannibal Expedition," they explained in broken French, "And we want to spend the night in your town." Whether their new friend had been self-appointed on the spur of the moment or was a genuine representative was incidental. He thought for a moment, bundled them all into his sports Citroen and before long had found a very suitable site. The old farmer who owned the land was most co-operative and actually took down a gate in order to permit easy access to the field. Cynthia stayed in camp, washing clothes for members of the expedition and preparing for the rush of many feet as elephant, team, Press and multitude would storm through the camp in order to reach the particular apple tree which Jumbo would have as 'bedpost'.

Richard and Baldi rejoined us and recounted a glowing story of how beautifully clean our linen was becoming in Cynthia's hands, also of the absent Mayor and how no one was expecting us at La Chambre. The prospect of a quiet evening with supper around the camp-fire was very pleasing. Until then, there was the 'caravan' to cope with. Pressmen flocked around us as we went through St. Remy and then passed over a level crossing. I have always thought that Colonel Hickman looked just the part as Veterinary Officer. However, one photographer asked him who was Monsieur Le Professeur of Veterinary. When he was told "I am", he exclaimed, "Good God !" and then proceeded to take photographs of him at every angle, putting on shoes, taking off socks, swigging lemonade, even just walking, rather in the same way that Jumbo's marching habits had been studied in minute detail. Quite when, and in what magazine this rather interesting series will appear is unknown but we all wait expectantly ! (While on the subject of the Colonel taking off socks, one cannot but mention his blister. He bore it nobly, especially as each day during regular inspections of Jumbo's feet, he must have wished his were in such fine condition. The success of the whole expedition pivoted on Jumbo's feet; if they failed, the expedition failed; if they stayed sound, then all was well. It was, therefore, reasonable to expect their mention in our first dispatch to Reuter. 'The Colonel reports that Jumbo's feet are in excellent condition. Jumbo reports that the Colonel's feet are killing him.')

We were rather late into camp that night. Cynthia had prepared a delicious dinner: salad, minute-steak and fresh fruit salad, and Jumbo's dinner was also waiting for her. Instead of really getting down to eat the one hundredweight of hay provided, as one might expect after a long day's walk, she had the most extraordinary habit of tossing it on to her back so that her appearance was more like that of a moving haystack than an elephant.

After supper we sat out under the stars, talking and laughing over the events of the last three days and discussing plans for the future. From under her tree twenty yards away ,Jumbo could hear our voices. We wished we could share our experiences with her for she seemed so human and we really were beginning to discover what a strong personality she had. Long after the others had retired to bed, Richard and I were sitting in the barn door with a Tilly lamp as near as we dared bring it without possible risk of fire. There was much to do, writing up the log and registering readings, making a public statement to Reuter, dealing with correspondence from all over the world and an idea which had come a few days earlier, preparing a printed programme for our proposed lectures in Turin and Rome. This would have to be ready by Saturday, when Richard was to make contact with our Italian Associates at Susa, keypoint on the journey and first large town over the frontier. Mr. Bateman, British Consul at Turin, Signor Terni and the Mayor of Susa would be waiting for him there and planned to discuss our arrival in Italy. The future had much in store for us but we were too tired to think what. We could only go to bed and laugh weakly before we went to sleep.

CHAPTER XI

Fourth Day's March

(Hannibal's Sixth from the beginning of the 'Ascent')

La Chambre to St. Michel

THE MAIN PARTY got off to a good eight-o'clock start. Jumbo had been keeping well to schedule and showed herself a good pace-maker for indicating the speed of Hannibal's army. Today she would have sixteen miles to cover along what almost certainly had been the Carthaginians' third days' unmolested march from the enemy town at La Rochette. Polybius relates that at the end of this time the army came to a town whose inhabitants welcomed the General with palms and pretended to be friendly. St. Michel fits well in this description for it stands at the junction of the Valoirette and Arc rivers and its history can be traced back to Roman times. The sixteen miles which we demonstrated would be a very probable distance to cover by the fast-moving army (in which elephants no doubt, set the pace) coincided with the relative positions of La Chambre and St. Michel.

It was going to be quite a hot day so, as the caravan passed through the town of La Chambre, we left Jumbo, by a fountain where it was certain that she would find endless amusement, and entered a shop to buy Ernesto a hat. After much hesitation and hilarity and in spite of the unanimous insistance that the expedition mahout should wear a turban, he chose a 'ten-galloner' which was our pride and joy for the rest of the journey. The touch of the Wild West fitted well into the general atmosphere of exploration. Michael, in his Indian *topi*, walking on the other side of Jumbo, further enhanced the scene. Some might not have thought this an exploration but we discovered it to be such. No matter how well you may know a stretch of highland country by foot, it will be entirely different if you chase an elephant over it. Why? Well for one thing, the people through whose land you pass will react to this unusual sight in most unexpected ways. Then there is the countryside itself. One looks on it from an entirely different angle. Will this bridge take the elephant's weight? How many elephant- hours away is the next town? Is this path suitable? Moreover, one's view is strictly limited for, unless one walks a good way behind, half the field of vision is now taken up with a vast grey-brown shape which gently heaves from one side to the other. No wonder, people have been known to be sea sick, not only whilst riding on an elephant but also walking beside it. A great mass of landscape keeps pace with you. This is all the more realistic as an elephant's, or, at least, our elephant's, back is a vast brown waste of heaving matter. The hairs stand out starkly on this desolate land of crinkled skin like burnt trees on some Paul Nash painting of 'A war- wrecked plain of France in the First World War'. Against this waste terrain is contrasted the fertile valleys, the dark pine woods and jagged snow-mantled peaks above. Yes, truly, if you want to have a new experience in holidays, take an elephant with you over one of your oldest haunts. You will find yourself on a mission of discovery. Wear a hat, to greet the occasion, either a ten-gallon or *topi* will do. We had both !

The road ran steeply down to the river over which a Bailey Bridge led to the village of St. Etienne. The Press had been rather slow starting today and photographers began to arrive well after nine o'clock. By that time we were following a narrow, deserted road, winding through silver birch woods and returning every now and then to the river. M. Alexandre, who was taking a cine film of the journey for television services all over the world, had been following us almost as closely as the two Paris-Match re- porters. Indeed he was often riding in the same car and the three now arrived to take some impressive shots of the elephant under a sheer, towering cliff which had had to be cut away for the road.

Then arrived a new reporter from Germany who went every-where on a Lambretta, Tim and David of Life and others. Whilst wondering where the Chronicle team had vanished we rounded a corner and saw Barber's car parked by a bridge. Stephen, himself, was gesticulating to a gendarme and, it appeared, both were quite hot under the collar. As we drew closer the argument subsided and Stephen turned to me. "This gendarme says that it's quite possible to cross this bridge and continue along the main road but that's rot. The place is inches thick with tar!" I jumped on a gendarme's bicycle and cycled across the bridge to investigate. He was quite right. In spite of various exclamations by the police that this was merely water being sprayed on to the road, my hand became a murky brown when I lifted it from the road surface and I pedalled back. Jumbo's feet would not possibly stand a good tarring at this stage of the game so we avoided the bridge and continued along a narrow track on the southern side of the river. Meanwhile, Press photographers had been making careful record on film of all deliberations and arguments !

We were due at St.Jean de Maurienne by eleven o'clock, for the Mayor had prepared a reception and had also promised that it would not take very long. Cynthia speaks better French than any- one else on the team so as we drew near this chief town of the whole Arc valley (called the Maurienne) she and I started to compose a speech of thanks to the Mayor. It was the only thing to be done. To start with my French is atrocious but to make make it worse, I had recently been to Germany for six months, so that often when groping for a French word, a German one would come out instead. However, with Cynthia's help a few reasonable sentences were thrown together and with speech in hand, untidily scribbled on the back of an envelope as we had gone along, I felt a better man as we entered the crowded streets. The Mayor gave us a warm welcome outside the town hall and introduced the team to all the local dignitaries who had come to town especially to be at the reception. Toasts followed and I was able, quite justifiably, to use the superlative adjectives on my scrap of paper in reply to the enthusiasm of the town. Normal, reserved, British thanks just fall flat in France. We were learning !

Another whole round of handshakes between the team and half-circle of dignitaries, with hands and arms criss-crossing in all directions and energetic dodgings to avoid collision concluded the half-hour visit and Jumbo and Co. were on their way. One old lady clutched my arm and said, "Are you in the Hannibal Caravan ?" "Mais, oui," I replied. "Is that an elephant over there ?" "Mais, oui," I replied. "Give him my love." "Mais, oui," I replied and had hurried on. I felt she meant it. There was something more than interest or sympathy on the faces of the townsfolk.

Lunch had been prepared by the Colonel. Military thoroughness and planning were at last replacing the rather haphazard methods of other team members. We were very hungry and parched with thirst when at two o'clock our party arrived at the spot the reconnaissance patrol had chosen. Everything was laid out perfectly. First, basin, soap and towel for the hands, then the food, spread out buffet-style on fruit boxes, and finally drinks, already poured into the odd collection of mugs, were standing on my guitar case. Ah, at last, a use for that guitar and case. Till then I had often wondered why on earth I had brought it. There simply had not been time to play. But now its existence had been justified. Groundsheets were laid out under a tree and we staggered over, with clean hands, an empty stomach, and a full heart.

Jumbo was travelling well and she had accustomed herself to the routine of daily marching and camping. There was little doubt that she was enjoying the whole business immensely. One could almost hear her saying to herself as we breasted the crowds at the entrance to St. Michel. "Oh, what fun. Another band, another Mayor, another grand reception. How I'll miss them all at Turin." But here our reception was rather different to Hannibal's. While the people of Ancient St. Michel had welcomed him, with united purpose to betray him, we on the other hand found the town split into two factions, one supporting the bandmaster and the other the Mayor. The latter wanted us to march to our camp site after the national anthems and two or three popular marches had been played by the band. The bandmaster, however, was indignant that so little of his talent should be exhibited and wanted to play on. There, right in the midst of an excited and pressing crowd I stood in between these two men who were going hammer and tongs at each other. What could I do! People wanted me to take sides, but before I could do so the bandmaster and supporters, shouting loudly and insistently, had their way. A salvo of military two-steps ensued and the Mayor shifted nervously from one foot to the other. At last the band considered that we had had enough for the time being and marched our elephant and us to the camp.

We had invited the Barbers, John Silverside and Timothy Green to dine with us that evening. David Lees had had to go off to Sicily to film opera. From elephants to opera seems a far cry but what head office says goes. Garibaldi, our cheerful lorry driver, had promised to cook us special Italian spaghetti and he and the girls were busy in the Quartermaster's area, huddled over primus stoves and, as was Garibaldi's custom, singing. Jumbo's cover spread on the grass white-side-up proved a magnificent tablecloth and with two Tilly lamps hanging above it from a rope stretched between two trees, the scene was set for a feast. Baldi's spaghetti was a huge success and dinner ended with ice-cream, fruit and coffee and we fell to talking about the future. Twenty yards away was the fence which kept out a little group of spectators who, even at this late hour were watching the diners and their elephant under the lamp- light. Quite suddenly the diners lowered their voices and one of them glanced over his shoulder to see if anyone was within earshot. There was a plan afoot—a secret plan which no one outside the assembled company should hear.

CHAPTER XII

Fifth Day's March

(Hannibal's Seventh)

Polybius Writes;

'The natives conspired together and came out to meet him with treacherous intentions, holding olive branches and wreaths which nearly all the barbarians use for tokens of friendship just as we Greeks use the herald's staff Hannibal was a little suspicious of such proffers of alliance and took great pains to find what their project and general motives were. They told him that they knew all about the capture of the town (La Rochette) and the destruction of those who had attempted to do him wrong and assured him that for this reason they were come to him as they neither wished to inflict nor to suffer any injury. Moreover, they promised to give him hostages from among themselves. Nevertheless, he hesitated for a long time, distrusting their word. However, reflecting that If he accepted their offer, he might perhaps make them more chary of attacking him and more pacific but if he refused they would certainly be his declared enemies, he finally agreed to their proposals and feigned to accept their friendship. Upon the barbarians now delivering the hostages and providing him with cattle in abundance, and altogether putting them- selves unreservedly into his hands, he trusted in them so for as to employ them as guides for the next difficult part of the road.'

[Note: To take into full account this important meeting and to fit our itinerary as exactly as possible to Hannibal's, we did not leave St. Michel until the following afternoon. It seems fairly reasonable to expect that when the Carthaginians stopped at this point, a considerable time was spent in assessing just how sincere were these friendly ovations. Moreover, it is certain that the soldiers were allocated provisions, so that for us to set aside the morning to cover such delays and, incidentally, for the expedition to have a much needed rest, was not only expedient but also historically accurate.]

We spent the morning in catching up on neglected portions of the log-book, shopping, reorganising the equipment and reading newspapers. Somehow, we had been brought into French politics and found that the intellectual, leftish weekly, L'Express, had got hold of the 'elephant story' and was using it as a source for satirical cartoons headed 'Vive L'éléphrancé'. They portrayed a variety of curious animals such as the gaullephant, which was sub- titled 'C' est beau, C' est grand, C' est genereux . . . L' éléphrancé ! ' parodying the General's famous utterance in Algiers last year. Two elephant book-ends, labelled Le Soustelephant, and Le Debrelephant were shown propping up copies of La Gangrene, L' Affaire Audine and La Question-three recent books on the sordid subject of torture in Algiers.

Then the Dauphine Libere gave us encouraging news from a French Army officer, Major Pierre Alixant. Practically half one page was taken up with his theory which I am pleased to say agreed with ours. The amusing side to the matter was that he seemed so anxious to retain priority for France in the discovery of Hannibal's true route. He claimed that in 1953 he had come across definite traces of an ancient road leading to the Col de Clapier which has not been mentioned in any reports of the region. I agreed with him when I read that the Clapier route had been pioneered years before by such fine French military historians as Perrin and Colin but not with his implication that "These English- men are not showing us anything new". He had somehow over- looked the massive, two-ton bulk of Jumbo. I laughed, threw the paper away and tossed off gym shoes, ready to clamber into heavier footwear for the climb ahead.

Old St. Michel is nearly two hundred feet farther up the side of the steeply sloping north face of the Arc than the present town. Until Napoleon's day there had been a huge lake in the area and it was not until he had broken the enormous natural dam that the ground where New St. Michel now lies, was revealed. We struggled up to the level of the old town, where no doubt Hannibal would have had to circumnavigate the lake, and having 'surfaced', the caravan took a narrow footpath to Orelle. At this point, the path divides, one route leading steeply downwards to the valley bottom and the other winding upwards towards a tiny village. The map was not very helpful here because it was so out of date. However, local guides had their opinions. All except one plump, unshaven peasant insisted that it would be impossible to take the High Road and that the only thing to do was to go down- hill. He, however, remained quite dogmatic, muttering, "C'est tres facile, Monsieur." He waggled the huge scythe drooping over his shoulder and looked indignantly at the others. Our constant companions of the road, two gendarmes on bicycles, were unhelpful. They had recently returned from North Africa and did not know the district well. We were still uncertain as to which route to take but clung on to the idea that our plump peasant might be right. I jumped on to the back of a Vespa belonging to one of the few pressmen who had followed us up to such a height and set out on a lightning reconnaissance patrol, leaving Jumbo drinking red wine and playing a borrowed harmonica. We were back in ten minutes and I gave the order to go ahead. The angry old women shook their heads and went back to their cottages. Our new guide, his sickle over his shoulder, led the way joyfully. Hannibal's local guides had been treacherous at this stage. How interesting that we should have to resort to the same methods as he. I only hoped that we would not be led over the edge of a precipice or into an ambush. The road narrowed, all cars gave up following us, and we passed through another and still smaller village. The look of complete and utter astonishment on the faces of the peasants was a delight to see. No wonder, for the village was very remote and I am sure that the news of Jumbo's travels had never reached this outpost.

The road was level now and Jimmy went ahead to see if a bridge over a torrent would hold Jumbo and then beckoned the caravan forward. There was a special technique in getting the elephant over any bridge because she was naturally conscious of her vast weight and would not easily commit herself to apparently fragile structures. No one else was allowed on the bridge for, if she were to side-step or try to turn around, one might easily get crushed against the railing or even pushed into the current. Then Ernesto would gently lead her forward while her trunk, extended to reach the ground ahead, felt the way to make sure it was safe.

Eventually, the path started to run downhill at quite a steep angle, one in four, and grew extremely narrow. Way down below, we could see the Press cars waiting. Even the kind Vespa rider had had to turn back and we made slow progress. The elephant's trunk is absolutely invaluable in such country and with it she was able to find good footholds with great certainty. Who said that elephants were only fit for the plains? Our jolly, peasant guide had proved himself correct. The High Road turned out by far the more interesting route and, certainly, more like Hannibal's than the Route Nationale.

La Praz is in the middle of nowhere, a lonely spot by a brook.

While we were trying to get there, Michael and the Colonel pitched camp, cordoned it off and were peeling potatoes and slicing beans. Why cordon it off ? You may ask ! Simply because, even out there in the wilds, the locals formed a 'Reception Committee' of excited youths who continually rushed through the camp making wild noises. One lad, probably a ring leader, pretended not to hear the Colonel's warning in French or, possibly, the Colonel's French is incomprehensible. Anyway, the Colonel then addressed him in German. Thereupon an old woman came up, determined that this was a German expedition and vehemently expressed what she felt about it. However, in time the Colonel quietened her. All's well that ends well, and I am told that finally she even offered to sing him an aria.

As soon as Jumbo had arrived, the centre of attraction was naturally switched from the camp to her so the road cordon was duly transferred. This took considerable trouble as it had to be out of the elephant's reach. That extra six-foot length of nose with which Nature had endowed her certainly added yards to the length of rope needed.

It suddenly grew dark, bitterly cold and started to pour with rain. The Reception Committee, adults and children, scattered, vanishing into the night with shouts and screams in their efforts to keep dry. We were left to face an angry wind which had suddenly veered and was driving rain in through the tent doors and an angry elephant who was tired, hungry, wet and unable to see. Everything had conspired against her and us. Why was it that on the one night that it rained we had arrived so near to sunset, the wind was so harsh and the food supplies had run out! Moreover, in the hubbub of arrival, Ernesto had somehow mislaid his most vital instrument, the ankus with which to control the elephant. Through the pitch-darkness, one could hear a huge, two-ton thunderbolt tearing at her chain and crashing through the under- growth. Then there came the wildest call I have ever heard, the trumpeting squeal of a near-wild elephant. It rose above the wind, it was carried urgently and impetuously up the valley and echoed back more faintly.

If that midnight fury had broken loose from her moorings and borne down upon the camp, there would have been very little left of either us or our equipment.

Cynthia and I, bent double in the hurricane, pushed our way through the lank grass to try and find a shelter for Jumbo, leaving Ernesto to deal with the elephant and the others to get all the equipment into tents and keep it dry. Clare had been sitting over a pot of soup coming to the boil on the primus at the wild moment of' wet darkness'. This she valiantly nursed throughout the gloom and cold while everyone else was rushing around, so that at the moment when we were all feeling most miserable, hot soup came to the rescue. Way down the valley we could see a light, so making for it found friendly farm folk and were directed to an open-sided barn which could take the elephant. With this happier news on our tongues, the walk back to the chaotic camp site was more pleasant, even though the rain now blew right into our faces. The narrow beam of my torch fell on the area around Jumbo's tree. It was a scene of complete chaos. Small trees which had been within her reach, now lay broken and splintered on the ground. The rope which we had so carefully placed out of reach of her inquisitive trunk, she had caught and twisted around herself It needed Ernesto's full patience and strength of mind to unravel that Gordian knot and quieten her down.

By this time, food supplies had arrived and we moved her to the barn. One cannot praise Ernesto too highly for the way he handled the situation that night. He was absolutely magnificent. The rain continued to pour down and the group of huddled figures, crouching over hot cups of soup in the dryest of the tents felt that they were experiencing at least some of the conditions the Carthaginians had faced.

CHAPTER XIII

Sixth Day's March

(Hannibal's Eighth)

POLYBIUS CONTINUES:

'After two days' march these same barbarians (who had been so friendly) collected, following on the heels of the Carthaginians, and attacked them as they were traversing a certain difficult and precipitous gorge. On this occasion Hannibal's whole army would have been utterly destroyed, had he not still had a little apprehension. Having foreseen such a contingency, he had placed the packtrain and cavalry at the head of the column and the heavy infantry in the rear. As the latter now acted as a covering force, the disaster was less serious for the infantry met the brunt of the attack. In spite of this, a large number of pack-horses and men were lost, for the enemy, being on higher ground, skirted along the slopes and either rolled down rocks or hurled stones by hand. This threw the Carthaginians into such severe peril and confusion that Hannibal was compelled to pass the night with half his force at a certain place defended by bare rocks and separated from his horse and pack-train whose advance he waited to cover. Next day he advanced to the summit the pass.'

From this narrative we can deduce various conditions for the placing of the ambuscade. (a) As the position had to be 'defended' by bare rocks, these would naturally slope downwards, away from the flat area of encampment rather than rise up around it. (b) There should be a large enough area for at least ten thousand men to encamp. (c) The summit of the pass over into Italy should be a day's march away. (d) It should lie on the second day's journey from the place the 'friendly' barbarians had met him. (St. Michel). (e) There should be a difficult and precipitous gorge.

Well now, much speculation has been made as to the location of this 'bare rock'. As I write, there lie beside me a pile of seven books, each propounding a different theory for Hannibal's crossing and each claiming a different 'bare rock'. Some translate 'bare' as 'white' from the original Greek and have found 'just the thing' that will fit the description. However, it has been decided recently that 'bare' is after all a more literal translation. But of all the 'bare rocks' which have been backed by the eloquence of classicists and military historians, I suggest that none is more striking or able to fulfill our five conditions than the rock at L'Esseillon.

So it was that on the sixth day of March we set out to reach this point of ambuscade. Richard left for his visit to Susa while the rest of us rallied round the elephant and set off along a winding path high above the northern bank of the Arc. It was a beautiful morning, the early shadows shrouding one half of the valley and the other bathed in sunshine. No traces of the previous night's terrible storm remained, except the loud rushing of brooks and the wet grass brushing against our bare legs. The caravan was now at the very southern-most point of the river's literal arc and a great head-land jutted its mass of rock southwards from the northern bank, shrouding us in its dark shadow. As we rounded this a completely new vista of the way ahead was suddenly revealed. The view faced straight into the morning sun and a winding line of silver indicated where the river flowed. Up beyond it, in the bright haze lay the outline of L'Esseillon and still farther, looking almost into the very sun itself stood the Great Cenis mountain group and the high lonely valley which led to Clapier. We paused for a moment and half-closed our eyes, imagining a mighty army of 40,000 men swarming up towards the bare rock. None of them knew what lay ahead. Hannibal had suspicions. One could almost hear him ordering his commanders to place the heavy infantry in the rear and the baggage train, elephants and cavalry ahead. The wheeling horses and lumbering elephants all taking their position in the great line of advance must have provided an unforgettable sight.

We set off downhill towards the last town of any importance this side of the frontier. Modane is not an elegant town. It straggles along the narrow valley floor and in places there is only one row of houses between its main street and the steep hill-side. It is from here that the railway has given up climbing and cuts straight through the high massif separating France from Italy in a ten-mile tunnel to Bardonecchia. We stopped for coffee in Fourneaux, the narrow suburb where the railway station stands. This is a good mile and a half downstream from 'old' Modane where we knew the Mayor and Corporation would be waiting for us but as the caravan was expected at eleven o'clock and it was now only ten- fifteen coffee would not be out of place. Parking is often a problem when you have an elephant in tow and, as we really wanted her to have coffee too, our area of choice was strictly limited. Moreover, it is no good leaving your elephant on the kerb for at least ten foot of clear way should be allowed between her and the traffic to accommodate the spectators. Otherwise there is bound to be a traffic jam and police intervention.

Three of us strolled into the cafe and lent on the bar. "Four coffees, please." "But you are only three ?" "We have a comrade outside." Pause. "Won't he come in ?" "She is too big." "Oh." Jumbo cupped her trunk and we poured in her tasse de cafe. There seemed hardly enough to drown a flea but she flung hack her head with great relish and shot it down a cavernous throat. What a mouth ! I had never seen it as finely displayed!

Teeth have never struck me as being particularly interesting. I never wanted to act on the suggestion once made to me that I should become a dentist, but elephant teeth are different and as no one is likely to suggest I become an elephant dentist I can speak of them with freedom.

Humans have three kinds of teeth, the incisors, for nipping and cutting, the canines for tearing and stabbing and the molars for grinding and chewing but with the elephant, things are a good deal simpler. He, or she in our case, is armed with two sets of magnificent molars. Is that all ? Well not quite. There are two surviving incisors which live in the upper jaw and have grown beyond all proportion, to form tusks. In a full-grown elephant, only two-thirds of their total length is visible, for the remaining third is embedded in the bone of the skull. Being only eleven years old, Jumbo's tusks are very small and moreover have been shortened in the Zoo. I have read of elephants with three or even four tusks but this condition is very rare. Now hack to the molars. The tusks are of no direct use in obtaining nourishment and all food has to he dealt with by the molars, hence the elephant's early specialisation in soft vegetable diets. Sometimes measuring over a foot in length the molars are enormous and weigh up to eight pounds. Jumbo's were somewhat smaller but nevertheless one cannot but be a little startled when the vast areas of tooth come into view. She was on the second set of four, but during her long (and no doubt illustrious) life she will have in all, twenty-four molars. Only one set of four, distributed so that there is one on each side of each jaw, is in existence at any one time.

While they are being worn down four new teeth are growing behind them. They slowly move forward replacing the old molars and eventually cast them altogether. The process then repeats itself. Perhaps I would not mind being an elephant dentist after all. Nature seems to do most of the work.

But we must hurry on, for the Mayor is waiting. Modane town hall was thronged with people and Jumbo made her bow, played the mouth-organ, much to the children's delight and then made for a near-by fountain. When I said, 'children' I really meant 'everyone' for we all become children at moments like this, so why not be honest ! The vin d' honneur was inside the town hall this time and we crowded up the wide, baroque staircase-a motley crowd of smart-suited V.I.P.s from the Customs, police, post office and local government, with team members in shorts, wind- jammers and dusty boots intermingled with bearded pressmen.

The speeches were short, the wine good and we were off again. A narrow cobbled lane from the market-place led towards the river. Operation 'bridge-crossing' was once again performed smoothly and we started a steady climb towards the 'bare rock'. The send-off from Modane had been tremendous but now crowds started to thin out and adults began thinking of lunch. Children are far more tenacious. Many a child has been known to follow our elephant long after the last adult had turned back with either tired feet, empty stomach or both. The Pied Piper of Hannibal did not need to make music to get the children following.

Jimmy Song stood back in the shadows and clicked his camera seven times. He had to work hard to produce all the photographs expected from him. The most onerous task was the production of a set of colour transparencies for each member of the team. As seven pictures come out better than six reproductions of one-the seven clicks. The shot he was now taking gave a fine view of the caravan, and the 'bare-rock' towering above as its giant walls blocked all but a narrow ravine of the valley. There is no doubt that one has to be fit when photographing such expeditions as ours. Jimmy was always on the move, when not actually clicking his seven times, then either catching up or going into position for the next shot. Next time we undertake a journey of this nature, the photographer will be provided with a Lambretta. As Hannibal never took a photographer a cameraman can be ear-marked as a modern addition and need not walk. Jimmy not only took some fine photographs but also walked, like any true Carthaginian. There was a huge cliff right ahead. A tiny figure stood at its summit and I watched John Silverside take a photograph of him.

"Who is that ?" I asked him. "Oh, it's the Paris-Match boy taking a shot at us ! "

The extremity to which these Press folk go ! It must have taken some climbing to reach that point-all for the sake of one photograph. Jimmy might have taken John taking the Paris-Match man taking Jumbo but the circle could never have been complete until we had trained Jumbo to work a camera and snap Jimmy.

90

The camp site for the night might well have been on the very ground from which Hannibal had defended his baggage-train and elephants. It was in fact on the top of the cliffs of the 'bare-rock' and had needed a steady and persevering climb to attain.

The late afternoon and evening were spent in rest and preparation. Just in case it started to rain again a barn was found near by to which Jumbo could be led. There was the noise of a motor and then right into the centre of the darkened camp shone a pair of blazing headlights. I breathed a sigh of relief At last we had back the expedition car. For nearly a week now it had lain in a garage of Central France with its radiator in pieces. Michael, however, had set off the previous night by train, cleverly avoided the storm which had caused such chaos in the camp and motored back with the old monster. It had come in the nick of time, just when its use would be most vital. We settled down to an early night. Why? Because next day the expedition would hit the trail at 2.0 a.m.

CHAPTER XIV

'Forced' March by Night

Hannibal's Ninth Day from the Beginning of the 'Ascent'

POLYBIUS WRITES :

'Next day the enemy made their departure. Hannibal joined his cavalry and pack-horses (and no doubt elephants) and advanced to the summit of the pass. He no longer encountered any large force of the enemy but was molested by a few now and then for some of them had taken advantage of the ground and attacked him from the front or rear.'

There was one problem which we had never solved during the 1956 Expedition and was very much in our minds during early planning stages of the 1959 journey. If the cavalry and infantry were able to cover the distance between L'Esseillon and the Col de Clapier in one day, it was doubtful if the more ponderous pack- train and elephants could have done it in that time. The climb is steep and winding. Moreover, the army would have to have been greatly extended in the narrow defiles and at places could not have been less than eight miles in length. But, before we left Cambridge, we had had an idea. One spring morning we had been studying the text with Dr. McDonald when Richard asked whether the pack-'train and horses might not have advanced during the preceding night, while Hannibal waited to defend the rock. Al- though this is not stated in the text, Dr. McDonald, studying the Greek text, saw no reason to deny that this might have been what happened. The idea began to seem more reasonable. There was no necessity for the baggage-train to wait under the gorge-surely it would have seemed only sensible to get the train free of such a vulnerable position. Then, it was clearly recorded that Hannibal's forces were divided and that he rejoined them next day, though it is not specified how the forces were divided.

This idea that the slower part of Hannibal's army had left the defile and was on its way to the Col by morning would solve the problem of his otherwise inexplicably rapid journey, and is our own original contribution to the study of the subject. It has not previously been considered-now we planned to try out the manreuvre on the ground with an elephant.

92

'A two-o'clock start might be alright if it is in the afternoon (as it had been two days earlier), but to get up and pack for an early morning trek at ·such an hour seemed madness.' Most of us were thinking this as we groped our way around the camp, searching for equipment and packing. However, to look at the other side of the picture, we were about to do something never attempted since Hannibal's day and the manœuvre was entirely secret, for the only people besides the team who knew were the Chronicle and Life correspondents. The world at large and of journalism in particular, would find the expedition, which they had been following so carefully, in a completely new and unexpected location next morning.

A late moon was rising above the mountains and the great rock faces of L'Esseillon shone in the eerie light. There was not a rustle from the trees which crowned the natural fortress and only the distant babbling of a brook finding its way down the steep slopes disturbed the silence of nature. The Colonel and Richard checked through the equipment we were to have handy: a compass, altimeter, pedometer, sandwiches and fruit, flambeau torches, Tilly lamp, chocolate, glucose tablets, large- scale map, matches and warm clothes. We were now ready to leave.

Ernesto's voice carried clearly from out of the shadows as he spoke in soft undertones. "Forward, Jumbo, forward, Jumbo, leg lift, lift, Jumbo, lift." When he had undone the chain which held her to a suitably stout tree, he threw it over her shoulder with a clatter and fastened it firmly around her neck. That chain could well be considered our most important piece of equipment. It had to be immensely strong as the elephant often pulled at her moorings during the night with enormous force and once 'adrift' she would be off under full sail. It was, therefore, a heavy chain and the only person strong enough to carry it was Jumbo herself. She wore it as some more sophisticated lady might wear a diamond necklace, rather than as a badge of servitude and seemed to entirely ignore its great weight. With a command from Ernesto, her huge bulk lurched out of the shadows into bright moonlight and I gave the word to start.

Even the Press had come ! Mind you, only the Press who knew what was going on. Tim and a replacement photographer, Pierre Boulat, of Life magazine, John Silverside and the Barbers arrived to see the camp being broken and then passed on down the steep, winding path to a gorge to prepare for photographs. The friendly rivalry between different sections of the Press was really amusing. Before Tim and Pierre had set out from the hotel, at I a.m. they left a note for the Paris-Match team who would have given anything to have been able to shoot the night's march. It ran something like this: 'Hope you had a good night! You have missed some good sport and will not find Jumbo at L'Esseillon if you fancy going to see.'

Down, down the tortuous path wound towards the valley floor below. The caravan slowly moved forward, Jumbo setting the pace and everyone eager to see how she would react to this unusual experience. Quite suddenly, we came to a narrow gorge where huge rock slabs rose on either side of the path. At one time, this was the only way up to the fort on L'Esseillon and so the rock had been laboriously blasted away to make the way wide enough for cannon and vehicle.

Here, the Press were waiting with flash-lamps at the ready and a merry word of welcome. Our flaming torches cast long shadows behind us and on to Jumbo's vast flanks and made the scene into as close a replica of the Carthaginian descent as any. Armour for us and the elephant was all that was lacking. There is little doubt that Hannibal's troops would have used torches of similar primitive design. We had prepared ours the previous night from instructions by the Colonel. Wooden shafts wrapped tightly with hessian sacking and fastened with wire strands from the bales of hay for Jumbo, had been left to soak all night in water, then at the last minute, just before our 2 a.m. departure, they were drenched with paraffin.

Hannibal had a further use for torches which we were not able to demonstrate. Later on in the campaign, when he had to cross the Appenine Mountains in Italy, Quintus Fabius Maximus was waiting by night to ambush him while he went through the only pass available. Hannibal outwitted the Roman by having lighted torches tied to the horns of a number of cattle and the herd driven in another direction. The Romans took the cattle to be Hannibal's men and the Carthaginians were able to slip through without casualty.

Our torches were almost expired by the time the caravan had reached the river Arc and we threw their charred remains into the whirling flood. Having crossed the river, there was a stretch of main road to cover before arriving at Bramans. Naturally, at three o'clock in the morning the traffic was somewhat thin. One or two cars came past, too fast to notice the unusual sight, but one motorist clearly had the fright of his life Jumbo and her party were keeping to the right of the road as the noisy machine approached from the other direction. The rider's head was bent forward, but as he drew near he raised it suddenly with wide-eyed amazement on his face. The machine swerved away from us, nearly hit the kerb and then shot off as fast as it could accelerate into the darkness. Perhaps that same day he was telling friends about the 'elephantom' which prowled the mountain roads !

At Bramans we turned right, off the main road. Our arrival here in 1956 had been somewhat different. The imaginary picture was the same, however; that of the thirty-seven elephants plodding upward in the darkness, but now it was more realistic. Even one elephant in tow makes a difference. The village lay still in the moonlight as we passed down its narrow, dark street. A pause at the village fountain for Jumbo's sake led to some good flash photographs and rather louder talking among the ranks than was really necessary. One old lady complained bitterly next morning to the expedition photographer of the noise which had woken her up. She received profuse apologies but these were to little avail as the root of the matter was disappointment. She had expected to enjoy the sight of Jumbo's approach in the blaze of a Sunday afternoon sun, and not as an elcphantom in the moonlight. If one newspaper report said, 'Jumbo was so quiet, she was able to pass through villages without waking anyone', this was not said by them all.

From the village, the road winds steeply and performs innumerable twists and turns. Jumbo was going magnificently in spite of the cold temperature and all the difficult conditions, never a murmur, never an audible comment; she just kept on walking, quietly, steadily and as softly as if on tiptoe. After a long climb of about one in eight, during which time Jumbo showed no slackening of pace, we stopped for a rest and 'breakfast'. It was not particularly appetising and we all felt extremely tired. However, the Colonel produced a small flask of brandy which bucked us up immensely and we moved off again in the grey light which would eventually turn to dawn.

Clare had been left a little way behind, writing up the log-book I believe, and in order to catch up she took a short cut over the top of a peninsula which we were circumambulating. As she slid down the steep bank towards the elephant, a stone was dislodged, but in no way dangerously. As soon as she heard the noise, Jumbo wheeled sharply towards it, with such speed that if anyone had been in the way he would have been knocked flat. It is well known that elephants have sensitive hearing but none of us knew that they, and Jumbo in particular, were so apprehensive about falling stones no matter how small. We learnt a lesson there and then which was to help decide a very difficult problem we had to face later that day.

The road was levelling now and we knew that most of the climbing for the time being was finished. Nevertheless, there still remained an extremely steep drop on one side of the path which had to be watched carefully. As dawn broke through the mist and started to drench the beautiful, high Alpine valley with golden sunshine, the expedition arrived at Le Planey. By this time, all feelings of tiredness had worn off and we were all for carrying straight on, up La Crosta towards Col Clapier after a couple of hours' rest. However, there was the Press to consider. It was Sunday and John Silverside would not be able to send his photo- graphs of this crucial section back to the Chronicle, because the transmission line was out of action at week-ends. Moreover, as far as the world was concerned, the expedition was still at L'Esseillon. It might be alright being one step ahead but two steps ahead could lead to a great deal of confusion and chaos. We decided to wait and conform to our initial plan of undertaking the night march on Sunday and the ascent of La Crosta to the Col on Monday.

By coming so far up the valley in the night march it was clearly demonstrated that Hannibal's elephants could easily have reached Col Clapier in a night and a day. Admittedly, he was attacked intermittently and probably had a more difficult path over the stretch to Le Planey, but we can make an estimated allowance for this and still find the distance well within his reach. It was not until we actually did the march to Le Planey by night that we were convinced it was possible. Richard Halliburton had taken an elephant over the Great St. Bernard Pass. If Jumbo had been as badly affected by altitude as his elephant, she would never have made it. Until now, all we had to go by, as regards unacclimatised elephants at high altitudes, was Halliburton's experiment. Work- ing by this, the distance between L'Esseillon and Clapier was far too great. We were hoping to prove high altitudes would not mean disaster.

Jumbo was hungry and the expedition's food supply had not yet come up the valley. At this stage, there is very little doubt that Hannibal's elephants just starved. While we were asking a farmer for some hay, Jumbo inquisitively poked her nose through a bed- room window. "Wakey, wakey," she could almost be heard to say. " It's high time you lazy people were up. We have been since 2 a.m. and are going strong." Two girls in thick, homespun night- dresses came to the window smiling, and we all laughed together.

It must have been a frightening experience, however, to see a twisting, snake-like object come feeling its way in through the window. Nevertheless, the discovery that it was Jumbo would no doubt be ample compensation. Anyway, the girls did not seem to be suffering from shock so that their recovery must have been immediate!

At this stage I might perhaps tell you about Dr. M. A. de Lavis-Trafford who has been described by journalists as 'The British Hannibalian Authority '. The first time that I had met him was at the Carlton Club where Richard and I were invited for a discussion of the problem of Hannibal. The Doctor is in his eighties but full of life and never in better form than when talking about Hannibal. As soon as the news of the proposed expedition had gone out over Reuter last February, he made immediate contact with us from his villa on the Riviera, 'Villa Lavis', and within days had sent each member of the expedition committee copies of the books which he had written on the Alps. Most of these were concerned with the very massif which we had studied in 1956, namely that through which the passes,

Clapier and Mont Cenis cut. More- over, one of them dealt exclusively with the problem of Hannibal's route. Here, clearly, was a man who knew the Alps. Indeed, for many years now the Doctor's hobby had been thoroughly to get to know the Cenis Range. Who's-Who put it another way by stating that his sports are 'Mountaineering, chamois-hunting and archaeology'. Our most exciting discovery from those books was that the Doctor's theory for Hannibal's pass coincided with ours. He gives his pass the name of Col de Savine-Cache, but really this is only a side exit from the larger Col de Clapier and not a separate pass. We had corresponded copiously during the following months and on the first day of the expedition, he had come to Montmelian with field-glasses, camera, sun-hat and car to follow our progress and give any assistance possible. He had been throughout most generous in giving us help and support and it was, therefore, not unnatural that at Le Planey the expedition should want to camp down by the river on land belonging to his chalet there. He gladly gave us permission.

As soon as the tents could be erected and sleeping-bags unrolled, team members crept in and slept. Meanwhile, the Press had started to arrive and were catching up on the news. The idea of a night march had taken them all completely by surprise. They took it well, laughed uproariously and saw the method in our madness; to emulate Hannibal's forced march.

Three of us went back down the valley in the expedition car to contact 'hostile Gauls'. In particular, we had to make peace with a Gaul who is amiable at normal times but on this particular morning was irate. I am refering to the Mayor of Bramans. By stealing through his village at dead of night we had disrupted all his plans for a full-scale Jumbo reception. I apologised profusely and made it clear that I knew nothing about these plans. We had passed through villages much larger and had had no reception. It all ended happily by the expedition inviting the Mayor and anyone else who would care to come to a vin d'honneur at Le Planey. The car raced down to Modane to get the best wine and then returned to the camp for lunch. From where was a poor, already heavily burdened expedition going to obtain wine-glasses for sixty people? For that is the number we reckoned would be present. Once again, Dr. de Lavis-Trafford came to the rescue. From the depths of his chalet-out they came . . . brand-new wine-glasses wrapped in straw. Together with the rather Bohemian collection of mugs belonging to expedition members, we just about had enough containers.

Jumbo stood quietly resting while trestle-tables were brought out—once again from that bountiful chalet-placed in front of her and, in due course, wine handed around. No Hannibal was ever faced with such a situation. Having been feted and invited to an endless succession of vin d' honneurs during the last few days we now reversed the process and were feting the general public in an apology for having disrupted their secret plans. Hannibal would have just killed them all and pushed on. We had been caught up in the complexities of twentieth-century publicity and lack of communications. With one matter happily settled to the tune of tinkling glasses and laughter, another more serious one took its place.

CHAPTER XV

La Crosta

THROUGHOUT THE AFTERNOON, pressmen and members of the expedition were exploring La Crosta, the only tricky part of the way ahead to the Col itself La Crosta means 'The Crust' and is the steep rock slope connecting the Ambin valley, on which Le Planey lies, to the six-mile-long valley leading to Clapier. The path is narrow and quite steep at places. After a meandering gently through woodland it strikes uphill and eventually has to resort to zigzagging in order to reach the level of the Col Clapier plateau. This plateau consists of the Clapier and Grand Mt. Cenis valleys, running parallel and at approximately the same height, between France and Italy, and the Col du Petit Mt. Cenis valley at right angles to these and connecting them. All this ground is over 6,000 feet above sea-level.

Bearing in mind that only the previous Monday the Colonel, Richard and Dr. May, a representative from the Zoological Gardens, Turin, had reported La Crosta in sufficiently good condition to allow the passage of Jumbo, it will surprise you that now some of us were beginning to have doubts about it. The reason was that there was now a new and entirely unforeseen psychological element in the situation. The build-up of the last week's journey had been enormous and world interest was at its height. Jumbo was no longer just an elephant. The question now was 'Would it be safe, within certain limits of risk, to take a world-famous elephant up ?' After supper the whole team set out for a final look at the ground.

Indeed, there were three problems which would require very careful handling. These we re-studied and there, standing on the narrow winding path with the last rays of the setting sun playing on the tree-tops we were still uncertain whether to take the necessary risk involved in bringing Jumbo triumphant to Col Clapier. There is no doubt that she could have managed it, if there were no disturbances, but the memory of her agitation at the falling stone which Clare had dislodged could not be kept out of our minds. The photographs the Press would take next day might well be by far the most exciting of the whole trip so that we could anticipate that the place would be swarming with photographers. If anyone climbed on to the rocks overlooking the narrow stretches and dislodged a rock, Jumbo might turn and cause a serious accident, either knocking Ernesto off the path down the slope or slipping off herself. Well then, you might say, "Couldn't you control the spectators ?" The answer comes "Yes, in theory, but in practice many photographers would be willing to risk their own necks and might be regardless of the safety of others in their efforts to get a truly spectacular shot." We were no longer in complete control.

Night had fallen and the slow, thoughtful procession climbed down to the camp. As we sat around with bowls of coffee, each team-member expressed his or her view of the situation. When all had been said I knew that mine would be the final decision. The topic of Jumbo herself came up and that is what possibly decided the issue. If there is anything we had learnt from the last week's priceless experiences it was that Jumbo as a person mattered. We had come to know her as a friend, as an untiring road companion, as someone who had gone through all our experiences, and had enjoyed the trip as much as we had. If now she could only add her voice to ours in giving opinion as to the feasibility of attempting La Crosta, the problem would be a good deal simpler, but there she stood, silent in the darkness, quietly swinging her trunk and munching supper.

It was her climb tomorrow that mattered-not ours. If a climber takes an estimated risk while ascending the Matterhorn and gets injured it is to a considerable extent, his own fault. He knows it and it is partly for this reason, the taking of decisions, of carefully calculated risks and then the success that follows which 'makes' climbing. With Jumbo it was different. Our decision might cause her disaster.

There was silence; then I turned to the others. "No, we won't go up La Crosta tomorrow. Another route to Italy will have to be taken." There now seemed complete unanimity in the team, and we were all prepared not only to stand by the decision, but defend it against the many criticisms inevitably levelled at us during the coming days.

The tension was broken and we tidied away the coffee things to go to bed. Nevertheless everyone was still thinking very hard.

Now, if we had been in a war or in anything like the situation facing Hannibal there would be no question in it. Jumbo would have gone up 'and she would have succeeded', I add bitterly under my breath. But how different was the situation for us. Ours was purely a journey of historical investigation. It was not vital that we climbed right to the pass. We had never claimed this to be our most important aim. Rather, it was to test our elephant on the day-to-day basis of Hannibal's march. This we had done. The eyes of the whole world were focused on the expedition. They knew that it was the 'big climb'. Moreover, animal lovers from every country were getting to know Jumbo as a personality. The news- papers had not been slow to paint as human a picture as possible of the dear, lumbering monster. The Societies for the Prevention of Cruelty to Animals poised for attack. We had always maintained excellent relations with them but knew that at the slightest opportunity they would pounce down our throats. It was not without a certain satisfaction that we were to hear the report of the Italian S.P.C.A. which, having thoroughly inspected Jumbo on her arrival at Turin stated that "She was in perfect condition". Hannibal had none of these issues to face. No Society for the Prevention of Cruelty to Animals existed in his day. He may have found his elephants almost human in intelligence and personality but he dared not treat them as such, but pushed them on, in a hectic relentless drive to the summit pass. There is nothing 'human' about that fantastic journey of destruction. It is only the attributes of courage, valour, military genius and determination which we admire in that great leader, not his humanity. No intrigued public was watching his progress with a personal interest and affection for the animals-only the Romans who would have been delighted if every single one of them had fallen down the ravine. No pressmen, within a minute's contact of Tokyo and Timbuktu, swarmed his way, quick to relay the slightest mishap. And I am glad. Dear Old Hannibal had quite enough to attend to. His was a far harder task and it took its toll. Out of 50,000 men only 30,000 reached Italy.

But then balanced against all this there were so many things. The public and Press would be terribly disappointed. The sheer sense of achievement and accomplishment if the ascent were tackled successfully would have been profound. It would be a fine tribute to the elephant, and to Signor Terni who had done so much to make our journey possible.

I found it difficult to decide which considerations were the most important, as I wearily went to bed that night.

CHAPTER XVI

Victory: over by Mont Cenis

POLYBIUS WRITES:

'After having a journey lasting nine days (from the "Ascent towards the Alps") Hannibal gained the summit pass. He camped there and stayed for two days to rest the survivors of his army and wait for stragglers. Meanwhile, a good number of the horses which had broken away in terror and some sumpter-animals which had thrown off their packs returned, strangely enough, having followed the track of the march and entered camp. As it was now almost the time of the setting of the Pleiades, snow had already settled on the summit. He noticed that the men were in a state of low morale owing to all that they had suffered and would suffer so called them to a meeting and tried to cheer them up. He relied chiefly on the actual view of Italy, which lies so close under these mountains that when they are seen together, the Alps stand to Italy in the same way as a citadel to a city. To some extent he restored their spirits by showing them the plane of the Po and reminding them of the friendliness of the Gauls there.'

Next morning there was movement in camp at five-thirty. Colonel Hickman, Richard and I were preparing for a Press conference ! "What ! At that time ?" you may ask. Yes, indeed, for had we been about to attempt La Crosta we would have to have started early and we had scheduled a Press conference for

6.0 a.m. in order to inform the swarming team of reporters and photographers exactly how the ascent was organised. The Colonel had been put in charge of operations and he was to give detailed instructions as to where the Press could go and when. However, all this was unnecessary since the decision of the previous evening. It had been made so late that we found it impossible to pass word down the valley that all pressmen could stay in bed.

Dr. de Lavis-Trafford had kindly said we could hold the conference in his chalet and there he was, at ten minutes to six, placing chairs in an orderly fashion around the great oak table and lighting the beautiful old brass oil-lamp.

The news was difficult to break. We all sat down, there was a moment's silence and as I glanced at the statement spread out before me it all seemed so unreal-especially at 6.o a.m. I shook myself. Had we really decided not to ascend La Crosta? Here it was in writing before me. That was sufficient evidence, wasn't it? I spoke quietly and the pressmen sat forward in their chairs in keen anticipation. The soft lamplight played on all, in benevolent impartiality. I briefly explained the problem set before us, the new element in the situation and of our late-night decision to circumnavigate La Crosta. I concluded that it in no way weakened the argument that Hannibal used the Col de Clapier, for this pass satisfied Polybius' description far too well. Colonel Hickman took up the train of argument and spoke in detail of the hazards of the ascent. After a brief period of answering questions we collected our papers and rose to leave. It was a signal for excited talking. Naturally, everyone was very disappointed but not more so than we were. The fact remained that these same gentlemen would be the first to criticise the expedition if any accident, no matter how slight, had occurred on La Crosta. Moreover, the more danger, excitement and hazard there was on that stretch, the better for them. This was not a principle we could hold to!

Outside were more pressmen and eager village folk who came clustering around. A mountaineer pushed his way through the crowd. He knew, he said, of another way up which would not cause any risk or difficulty. A local gendarme vehemently disagreed with him and started an argument. Maps were brought and the path pointed out. Half-way back to Bramans there ran a steep valley northwards up the fierce rock buttresses of Mont Belle-combe. Following this was a path which crossed the high ridge linking Bellecombe and Mont Froid at nearly 9,000 feet. It then descended to the entrance of the great valley which terminated in Clapier. If there was the faintest chance of our using this ingeniously thought-out route and not having to return to the Arc, every effort was worth making. Within minutes a reconnaissance patrol was formed. Of the team there would be the Colonel, Ernesto and myself. Our local guides would consist of the bright-thinking mountaineer and two frontier police. As we set off down the valley after only the scantiest of breakfasts, we were light-hearted and ready for anything. The dawn had come in its full glory now and the valley filled with magic light. Our path looked hopeful. However, as we climbed, the sheer length of the ascent began to strike us. It just went on and on and on at a gradient of one in four. There were tricky parts but these could all be put right with a little careful preparation. No, it was the ruthless, sheer, dogged climbing which eventually made us collapse on to the green sward, talk the matter over for a few minutes and then decide that Jumbo should not go up here.

Crestfallen we returned. But, as compensation public trying-on of Jumbo's boots caused much interest and merriment in the team and among the Press. One Paris-Match photographer actually tried them on himself, with legs and arms in each of the four. We took pictures of him, crawling into the biggest shoes in the world, and suggested he acquired elephantitis to obtain a good fit. Jumbo seemed quite happy with them on but clearly preferred not to wear them unless it was absolutely necessary. The original idea of bringing boots had come from the Curator of Mammals at London Zoo. Throughout the journey it always proved wise to have them present for they might have to be used for certain specialised types of emergency-such as when a flood had washed away the road and left in its place a rough rocky surface which could cause damage to the elephant's feet. In reality we never had to use them and it is a nice question whether, at any crucial stretch, the time lost fitting the boots on properly was more valuable than the damage to the feet did not once have to bother us.

The return to Bramans was the limit to any retreat we had to undertake. It was pleasing to know that the one village which had never been able to see Jumbo, due to the night march, had her now passing through in broad daylight. From here we turned north-east, struck up-country towards the Pass of Great Mont Cenis and by evening had reached Termignon, well upstream from Bramans. This small town is at the very base of the steep ascent planned for next morning. The reconnaissance patrol had contacted the obviously very surprised Mayor, procured a camp site outside the town and a barn for Jumbo.

Looking at the alternative routes connecting the Arc to the Dora Ripario basin in Italy, the Col de Clapier and the Col du Grand Mont Cenis stand out as by far the most significant. Of the two, Clapier is the more direct route. On the other hand, it is a good deal higher. Before Napoleon had built his road across Mont Cenis there could not have been very much to choose between them. Apart from the short stretch on La Crosta, Clapier would have been easier on the ascent than on the descent. Mont Cenis had a long steep climb from the Arc and a fairly easy descent to Italy. Hannibal almost certainly sent his troops through both passes though probably he himself and the elephants used Clapier.

As we carefully planned our assault on the Mont Cenis pass that evening, we tried to imagine it as it had been in pre-Napoleonic days, a path wide enough for a cart or chariot but no more. Today, of course, there is the main motor road up the steel valley-side, zigzagging in broad easy sweeps up the 2,000-foot climb, though progressing only a mile and a half as the crow flies. However Hannibal would not have had the use of such luxurious climbing. One of the oldest routes to the Col left the tarmac at Termignon and struggled up the mountain-side as a mere cart-track through high, wild country to nearly 7,000 feet. Does this not show why Clapier might have been preferable to Hannibal? Not only was it the shorter route but also, taking an overall view, the gentler ascent. Admittedly, the steep ascents above Bramans and at La Crosta each climb for a thousand feet, but by taking the climb in two stages with the easy-going Ambin valley in between, this would probably have seemed easier to Hannibal than doing the full 2,000-foot ascent necessary to reach the Mont Cenis pass. If our path had gone straight up, its gradient would have been less than one in three. This was the ideal path to take, away from any motor traffic and a stiff enough challenge for any elephant. Steven Barber and the Colonel had gone over it the previous day and claimed it was passable.

I do not know where the word Termignon comes from but to me it has always implied Terminus. At least that is the best way to remember the word and moreover it was, indeed, our terminus as far as the week's progression up the Arc was concerned. The expedition contingent which accompanied the elephant through the deserted streets of early morning saw little sign of life save the odd scavenger dog nosing its way through the refuse of back yards and one or two industrious housewives, pausing for a minute to see the strange caravan pass.

The rest of the team set out to pay homage to a great man. It was appropriate that on the one day the Mont Cenis and Clapier passes should be attacked simultaneously. While Jumbo was steadily climbing through thinning pine-woods to above the tree-line, members of her following had taken a strategic leap ahead by the main road in the expedition car, and were already well on their way to the Col de Clapier on foot. They had avoided La Crosta by cutting across country from the Grand to the Petit Mont Cenis Pass, and from there, climbed up the uneven valley at over 7,500 feet above sea-level to Clapier.

Their homage was to be made to Hannibal; to stand where he stood, to point to the clearly defined Po valley, as he had done and to address the ' troops'. The fact that it was impossible for our elephant to stand by did not deter them. There was a challenge to be issued, also; Stone-masons had come up from Modane and carved our elephant in the rock for the occasion. But there was no inscription. It was left for the first team who might bring their elephant to this very spot to complete it.

Can we pay sufficient tribute to our elephant ! That day she climbed magnificently. The weather had clouded over somewhat and there were two squalls of rain; however, it brightened up by twelve noon and the photographers got to work. For them, this was the highlight of the journey. No wonder they grew excited. Beyond the huge pachyderm, steadily climbing higher and farther from the deep forests and valleys, lay ranges of magnificent peaks. The great glacier of the Vanoise, stretched across the far horizon, presided over a panorama more than spectacular. I show my friends a photograph of Jumbo passing over a typical bridge along that route. They almost all gasp and then cry, "Didn't she collapse it r" Fortunately no ... !

However, it was something to be on the guard against. A two and a-half-ton heavyweight, very mo- bile and able to reach places no four-wheeled vehicle would dare approach, could do serious damage-to herself as well as the 'Mountain furniture'.

We crossed the watershed, the Col du Grand Mont Cenis, 6,893 feet above sea-level, at 2.0 p.m. Over the ridge lay the Mont Cenis plateau with its magnificent lake and the ruined hospice Napoleon had founded. The drop to the lake was not very great, a mere 500 feet, and we sauntered down the easy road in high spirits. In one sense, it was the first time I really relaxed since the night march. The last few days had been heavy with problems and urgent, important decisions. But now, we had made it, or rather, Jumbo had made it. The way ahead was clear and life seemed full of bright horizons. The cluster of television photographers, pressmen and others which had hailed the caravan with excitement at the summit disappeared. There was peace on earth. As we walked we chatted and joked. Ernesto was radiantly happy and one feels that his spirit infected Jumbo. She fairly sailed down- hill and it needed a smart pace to keep up. Poor Ernesto, he had had a grim time. Not only was his engagement ring lost at La Chambre but also, the lady of all our dreams had done her worst. At Termignon, 'while all men slept', she had suddenly sprouted those horns and forked tail for which she is notorious and not only trampled on most of her trainer's equipment but actually eaten a pair of trousers and a shirt. But now he was on the crest of a wave, had put away the memory of the hurricane at La Praz, thoughts of a futile search in the grass for a ring and the remains of a shirt which were not even worthy of wiping Garibaldi's windscreen.

Beneath us lay the lake, still and blue, and upwards soared mountains in great generous sweeps of grandeur. Surely, life was good. I turned to God in a few short minutes of adoration and thanks.

A group of old, weather-beaten houses down by the lake (and along the main road) indicate where stand the nearest 'hotels' for miles, horizontally and thousands of feet, vertically. We stopped here, not that we wanted to stoop to hotel living but because a huge barn-cum-garage would prove the ideal place for Jumbo. This was to be her highest night ever and the risk of her catching an elephant-size chill was not worth taking-jacket or no jacket. Cars were driven out and in moved Jumbo.

The expedition camped down by the lake a good half-mile away. Everyone was too tired to think of cooking food or of eating it by primitive means so we left the whole lot, trusted that there would be no thieves at such altitude and all seven of us piled into the car to return to the huddled hotels and Jumbo. Ernesto and Garibaldi were already happily installed in Jumbo's barn, with free meals at the hotel and were surrounded by a cluster of excited Italians listening to their spell-binding story over cups of coffee in the bar. We left them to it for they must have been so happy to return to the borders of home territory. Neither had been able to speak French and were now loosing their tongues at last. Michael and Jimmy motored down to Susa to get some photographs enlarged for the next day when we wanted to present at least the skeleton of an album to the Mayor there. The rest of us went noisily into a restaurant and sat down to the most magnificent dinner a celebration of Jumbo's achievement could warrant.

It was pitch-dark and pouring with rain when we finally emerged. As the car had not returned we walked back to camp with faces stung by the lashing rain and hair swept back. The camp was in chaos. The girls' tent leaked anyway and now the rain and wind had seeped in everywhere. Fortunately a near-by barn pro- vided much-needed refuge. Richard wanted to stick the night out in a tent but the Colonel, Clare, Cynthia and I gathered together a few essentials and rushed barnwards with maximum speed. Any discomfort or misery was completely overwhelmed by the joy of having arrived 'over the crest'. The day's victory eclipsed the present drastic defeat inflicted by the elements. For the first time in 2,177 years, an elephant had successfully climbed the Alps.

110

CHAPTER XVII

Descent to Italy

WEDNESDAY, THE 29th July had dawned. Our camp at nearly 7,000 feet above sea-level had been extremely cold that night and more than one team member complained of his sufferings from the icy wind. But now, the morning stood bathed in sunshine and there was that exhilarating tang in the air which only comes after a night of heavy rain. The early morning breeze, rising briskly from across the lake played through our hair as we prepared to start the downhill trek.

The speed-time section of our log-book was virtually closed now that we had breasted the summit, for our original plan had been only to study the nine days of Hannibal's ascent. Nevertheless, as we set out from Jumbo's ham I still took readings and entered them in the log-book which, by now, was looking very dilapidated. It would be interesting to see how the elephant reacted to long, steady declines.

The road ran along the side of the lake, past Napoleon's ruined hospice and then slightly uphill to the edge of the Mont Cenis Pass plateau. From here, as from the pass itself, three miles back, a fine view of the surrounding mountains was given but nothing of the Po valley at the foot of the Alps. Only Clapier and Traversette give this view. After a minute's pause, we plunged down towards the frontier post.

The elephant's passport was a makeshift affair with a white cardboard cover, taken from the bottom of a sweet carton, and leaves provided at the crucial moment by Alexandre, the TV cameraman. However, it was elephant-size, and made interesting reading.

Number of Passport/No. Du Passeport — 2177 (the number of years since her forebears had crossed with Hannibal).

Name of bearer/Nom du titulaire — Jumbo, otherwise called Hannibella

Accompanied by his wife (maiden name)/Accompagne de sa femme — No; she *is* a lady (neé)

Age/Age — 11 years

112

Nationality/Nationalité — Indian

Place of Residence/Residence — The Zoological Garden, Turin.

Profession/Profession — Mountain climber and builder of trunk routes.

Height/Taille — 8 feet 6 inches.

Colour of eyes/Coleur des yeux — Brown

Special peculiarities/Signes particuliers — A long nose and a partiality for pears!

Usual signature of Bearer/Signature du Tatulaire — N.B. Even an elephant-size passport is not large enough to take an elephant-size footprint!

At the frontier post she behaved beautifully, would not have objected if the Customs had wanted to search her and went so far as to personally hand her passport to the frontier policemen, for inspection. At the crucial stage we thought she would eat 'it, as she had eaten Ernesto's shirt, but it landed safely into the hands of the smartly uniformed official. He stood to attention, looked it through and having ascertained that this really was the young lady with a long nose, stamped it with great ceremony and handed it back to her. Jumbo dutifully passed it on to her keeper muttering, one would imagine, under her breath:

"Take this, friend! I've no pockets."

The thought occurred to me as the Customs officials beamed on our party and waved us on that no better means could have been devised for smuggling. If what you want to smuggle is liquid, such as rum, then your elephant's ten-gallon reserve tank could be used. If it is long and thin, there is always her trunk in which to hide it and if it is anything else just carry it with you. No one would notice it, for all the world would be looking at the elephant, admiring her, vigorously stamping her faked passport and shouting with delight. Having lifted the barrier with her trunk and posed for an ever-increasing number of photographers she passed on into her homeland-Italy.

The reconnaissance patrol had one final task to perform before resigning for the season. This was to prepare a celebration coffee-party en route.

I will return for a moment to a conversation in Birmingham. I was speaking to George, an old friend of mine, deeply involved in the confectionery business. Unfortunately he would be unable to come on the expedition, so he said, but there and then promised to supply anything we would need in the cake line. The result was the order of an elephant cake. But, alas for its pristine glory- trouble began when our car had broken down. The cardboard carton with its delicate and artistically executed contents was among the many and varied objects, first thrown into the garage lorry, then into the train, then on to the station cart at Montmelian. Since those early days the poor old oversize cake had survived countless moves, two thunderstorms, the weight of an elephant boot and the hungry glances of a wide variety of people—including Jumbo. Pieces icing had flaked off, there was a dent in its tummy, a tusk had fallen away and without doubt it looked a sorry sight. But now it had come into its own. By the time the caravan arrived at the appointed roadside cafe, the magic, heated knife of the proprietor, dressed in white apron and tall chef's hat, had worked miracles. There was the elephant cake, our poor be-nighted elephant cake-as good as new ! Never was there a coffee- party like that one. We sat in the sunshine with the chef beaming at us from his doorway and Jumbo's inquisitive trunk dangling down into the centre of our little circle of friendliness. She was obviously very interested in this cake: so much so that after a first helping, of its trunk, she insisted on a second before others had had their first. We meekly agreed for after all, this was in her honour, but made sure that at least some was turned over to the humans of the party.

There was plenty of time before our scheduled arrival at Susa, first town in Italy, so we found a shady dell and relaxed. A Finnish radio

114

producer arrived and made recordings of the team. At all kinds of odd moments since having crossed the Col, various microphones would be pushed under our noses and statements demanded. Some inkling of the sort of reception that awaited the elephant was dawning and I was beginning to get worried over my non-existent Italian. Fortunately, our interpreter for the Susa visit had motored up to give us the low-down on preparations. He was a youthful student, bubbling over with enthusiasm and continually referring to our evening's host as' My Lord Mayor'. Together we composed a speech in Italian to thank the Mayor for what would undoubtedly be a superb reception. Then we carefully went through the pronunciation and when he had gone I sat with vacant eyes saying the strange words over and over again. The humour of it was that at exactly the same moment 'My Lord Mayor' was industriously learning his English words of greeting. Picture the situation. An English engineer with elephant near by learning a strange little speech of anticipated thanks while 2,000 feet beneath, an Italian schoolmaster (as I later discovered he was) memorising an equally strange mumbo-jumbo. Neither could speak the other man's language.

We eventually set out for the town and saw what Jumbo could do on gentle, steady declines. Her consistent five miles an hour made unusual reading in the log and, indeed, it was hard work stopping to enter the readings and then having to catch up.

Any ideas of what would happen on descending the last 2,000 feet to civilisation were completely dwarfed by the stupendous welcome only the Italians can give. Susa was absolutely jammed full of people. The farm folk had come in for miles around and to claim that the population of what is really quite a small town had suddenly swollen to three times its normal size is no overstatement.

A huge banner spelling out' Welcome, Jumbo' portalled the town entrance and the crowds closed in around us. Here, walking up to meet us were the Mayor and Mr. Bateman. We warmly shook hands. The Mayor looked into my eye and I into his and simultaneously our hearts fell at the thought of the gruesome ordeal of speech-making. Weeks later, after all the team had gone home and I was wandering over the Alps at leisure we were to meet for morning coffee in the town square and laugh over the whole matter. Then came the dancers, in their bright regalia and the band, in full blast. The excitement, animation and enthusiasm of the milling thousands have printed a picture on our minds which we and Jumbo will never forget. One doubts if a more rousing time could have been had even if our elephant had climbed Everest!

Having been made honorary member of the Alpini—Italy's exclusive mountaineering club, with the ceremonious presentation of alpine hat and medal by the local president, Jumbo was led to the cathedral square and fed with carrots from a bright orange monster. It was the pride of the town-a brand-new ditch digger with the trade name Jumbo written in bold letters across its flanks. Then came a great honour, the greatest Susa can offer, I am told. Our elephant was solemnly led through the famous triumphal arch. It had been erected by King Cozeo, for his Emperor Augustus, 2II years after Hannibal had passed that way, in 7 B.C. From there the long procession passed to the town hall and while Jumbo was being taken through palatial gates to a courtyard where she could reside in complete luxury, we were whisked up to the Mayor's parlour for speeches and presentations. The Press and local dignitaries crowded in.

SUSA

I must say that the Mayor said his piece in English better than I mine in Italian and I can't really make the excuse that he had had

116

more time to prepare. Our reception was too magnificently and meticulously arranged for that to be so. After a further long speech in Italian he presented the two lady members of the expedition with dolls in local costume and I rose with weak knees and a stammering tongue. If not eloquent, then our thanks were at least sincere. Then Jimmy's hard work of the previous evening came into its own for we were able to present to the Mayor an album of expedition photographs.

There was one more thing I wanted to say so I called over our enthusiastic student interpreter to assist. It ran something like this: 'Hannibal had crossed the Alps on a mission of death and destruction, of hatred and revenge. Could we not contrast that terrible journey with Jumbo's which, we hope, has brought only happiness and friendship ? One of the most unforgettable memories of the journey has been the light of joy which lit up faces of children and adults alike—all the way along the route. But all is not peaceful nowadays. The world lives under the threat of atomic warfare. Ballistic missiles are the fear of the day. That which was launched at Montmelian and which has now landed safely in home territory with, we suspect, only constructive effect has been a peaceful intercontinental Hanniballistic elephant !'

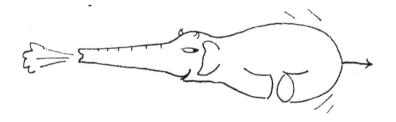

Hotel rooms had been booked and after settling in we strolled over to the restaurant on the other side of the square to watch our- selves on television. It was an extraordinary sensation thus to see our arrival in Italy twice over. Things I had not noticed at the time now stared me in the face. I saw, for instance, that Clare had been wearing her hat at an extraordinary angle, that that humorous little French photographer who used to be with us at the beginning of the journey had returned and that my own hair had been shockingly untidy.

The reception dinner was even better than our celebration feast up on the Pass the previous night and instead of returning to a chaotic camp site drenched with rain, we went for a moonlight stroll in the ancient Roman quarters of the town. Our ever-present interpreter talked at length of all the historic glories of this fascinating town but most people were too tired to take it all in and just enjoyed being alive.

However, we certainly did not feel nearly as tired as the Carthaginian army which Polybius describes as being in 'wretched condition'. He writes:

'Having arrived in Italy Hannibal camped straight away at the very foot of the Alps to refresh his men. (Very probably this spot was Susa.) His men had not only suffered severely from the difficulties of ascending and descending the passes but were, moreover, in a terrible condition due to the lack of provisions and the neglect of their persons. . . . They had become more like beasts than men. It was for this reason that Hannibal took great pains to attend to the men and horses until they were restored in body and spirit. When his forces had regained strength he contacted the Turini who lived at the foot of the mountains in order to win their friend- ship and alliance. However, these overtures were rejected, Jor the tribe had quarrelled with the Insubres (a tribe farther east, allied to Carthage). Hannibal besieged their chief town (very probably on the site of the present Turin) and captured it in three days.'

Two days after our descent into Susa the caravan entered Turin. Jumbo had come home and the reception she received was completely different from Hannibal's. I could go into another enthused description of the crowds, the band, the complete traffic disruption, and general cessation of all work till the 'elephantessa' had passed, but I need hardly do so. Let your imagination do the work. Only remember that this was bigger and better than ever. A hundred yards before arriving at the Zoo gates we persuaded Ernesto to mount the elephant he had so patiently led a full hundred and fifty miles. Till then, he had walked every step of the way and if any person should share in the glory belonging to a certain pachyderm it was he. Through gates of splendour decorated with welcome signs he rode her and on into the elephants' enclosure.

Everyone who ever mattered in international circles at Turin was there at the dinner that evening, from the Mayor and the British and French Consuls downwards. I sat between Mr. Bateman and a

118

Roman Senator Senator Sibille held strongly opposed views on Hannibal's route and we had already had a long correspondence. Long ago I had anticipated that if we ever met the most animated discussion would ensue. He held the theory that Hannibal had gone over three passes; the Col de Mont Genevre, and the subsiduary passes of La Scalla and Bousson. No wonder Signor Terni, who had so lavishly arranged the dinner, made us sit together. From across the table his amused face was watching the glint of battle in our eyes. Long, long the battle raged amid mild interjections from Mr. Bateman's side between each round. The end of the contest consisted of a warm invitation from the Senator to visit his mountain chalet. He himself would personally conduct me over the three passes. I accepted gladly and we fixed a date.

Picture the scene two weeks later, when, having viewed the passes together we motored to Guillestre in the French Alps and visited an old friend of the Senator's, General Guillaum. The General held to the Traversette route, so that what with the Senator and I each pumping his own line the afternoon's discussion was far from dull. At the end, we all laughed and suggested that so many people worth knowing were interested in the Hannibal problem, an international congress on the subject should be organised to bring them all together. I started to count on my fingers who might be there. Well, to start with, how about Dr. McDonald and Sir Gavin de Beer? Then, while still thinking of the British Isles, we could invite Sir John Hunt, who had written me the two amusing letters on 'oxygen for elephants', Dr de Lavis-Trafford of Le Planey fame, and Colonel John Hickman to lecture on elephants.

From France would come the General, Major Alixant who had so opportunely supported the Clapier theory and possibly Gilbert and Colette Charles-Picard whose recent book La Vie Quotidienne a Carthage au temps d' Hannibal is extremely enlightening. Italy's delegates would be Senator Sibille, of course, and Professor Vittorio Morone, of Susa and Turin, who was a magnificent mountaineer and knowledgeable classicist. By chance I met him two days later, in a Susa coffee house. Our mutual interest, Hannibal, was so strong that I ended up by spending the night in his home, after examining the ancient sources well into the early hours of next day. An invitation to go chamoix hunting in late October and climb up to Clapier in the snow has had to be regretfully declined. This book is taking too long !

From across the water would come Victor Mature, who is as interested in Hannibal as anyone I know. When we met in Rome he was dressed as the Carthaginian leader in the Warner film production and had not a little to say about the question. Also there would be Mr. Power, a Californian I have long wanted to meet. His book Hannibal's Elephants is widely used in American schools as background for classical history lessons. Germany would send my old friend Dr. Muhlmeister, of Hanover, who had presented to the expedition two magnificent prints of old drawings showing Hannibal's crossing, and Professor Chien Hsuin Yui whose house at Dusseldorf is full of ancient Roman and Carthaginian relics. It is clear that the question of Hannibal is not just the interest of the seven in our team. No, it is fascinating to many and much greater men than I.

But to return to our dinner-table at Turin, the time had come for presentations and speeches. The Mayor received an album of photographs of the expedition. Two huge parcels were lifted forward and in due course handed to Signor Terni. The first contained Jumbo's famous passport and the other her boot. One felt now, as the finel of our drama was drawing to a close, that of all the cast surely Signor Terni deserved the most curtain calls. When he had heard our plan to support Refugee children with the proceeds from the expedition he acted spontaneously and provided not only an elephant free of charge but also loaned Ernesto and Garibaldi, provided a lorry, petrol and sufficient food to keep Jumbo going for some time!

Our last album of photographs was for Mr. Bateman. In the front rested an illustrated parchment with the words—'To Mr. E.C. Bateman, with many thanks for finding us an elephant to take across an Alp in search of one-Hannibal'.

My mind went back to the foggy December evening in Birmingham when, having returned late from work I opened his first letter to me. It read as follows:

'Dear sir,

'Unusual as your request may be-well, unusual I should perhaps say for a Consulate, I am happy to inform you that I have been able to secure an offer of an elephant for your projected crossing of the Alps next summer.'

Fine words to launch the journey which now drew to its close.

120

Under a star-studded dome the team went over to the elephant stables to say good-bye to the centre of all the attention. There was a journey she would never forget, even if she had not been an elephant!

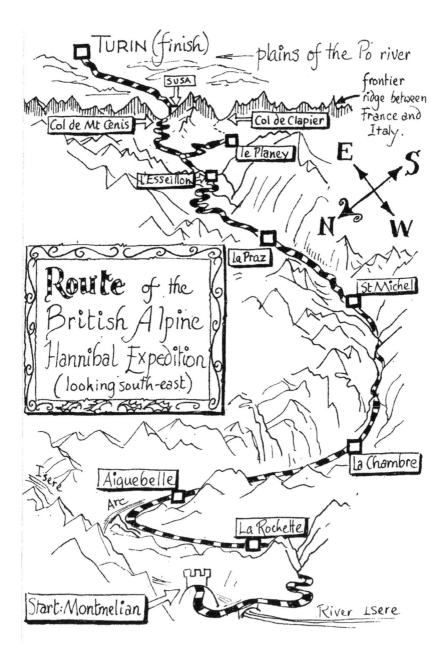

TURIN (finish)

plains of the Pò river

SUSA

frontier ridge between France and Italy.

Col de Mt Cenis

Col de Clapier

le Planey

L'Esseillon

E

S

N

W

La Praz

St Michel

Route of the British Alpine Hannibal Expedition (looking south-east)

La Chambre

Isere

Aiquebelle

Arc

La Rochette

Start: Montmelian

River Isere

PART THREE
AFTERMATH

CHAPTER XVIII

Elephant

"OH—TELL ME another, I don't believe it!"

We were having one of our few leisurely discussions at a time when the expedition was in full swing and we had time to sit around in the evening. It was getting dark. Ernesto stood up to light the Tilly lamps and said: "Yes, honestly. Somebody once said 'An elephant's life is one continual meal'. That's not far from the truth."

"What interests me most is the trunk. When you really think about it, an elephant would be pretty helpless without it."

"It's just an elongated nose, I suppose." "And an enormous upper lip."

"No, I disagree, an elephant doesn't have an upper lip at all.

If he wanted to grow a moustache, he couldn't for there would be nowhere to place it. But think how useful that nose is ! Instead of needing a very keen sense of smell in order to diagnose all the odours which surround him, the elephant can literally place his nose on anything and although his head is six feet off the ground, can examine it at very close quarters."

"They say that the trunk is a bundle of nerves." "Oh, I wondered where that phrase came from!"

"Yes, and with this complicated network of nerves connected to the tip, and hundreds of hairs growing on its inside, he can tell the shape, texture, temperature and edibility of any object touched."

"You know it's funny but until I met Jumbo I had always thought an elephant drank through it's nose."

"Most people think that too."

"I suppose the elephant is the only animal that has to use her nose to lift water to the mouth. Her neck is too short and inflexible."

"But why is her neck so short and inflexible ?"

"Because it has to carry the heavy weight of that trunk—the water-lifter."

124

"Oh, I see. It's a kind of pleasantly vicious circle!"

"What she loses on the swings, she gains on the roundabout. Look how useful that trunk is! It assists drinking and eating, and can be used for shooting sand over herself, blowing the flies away, lifting things and people, pushing, pulling, making noises and expressing her affection."

To change the subject slightly Cynthia flung out the question. "But tell me, what are the differences between an African and an Indian elephant ?"

Everyone joined in with ideas and, of course, the first one concerned the ears.

"An African elephant has large ears while Jumbo, being Indian, has small ones."

"Does this mean that the African has better hearing than the Indian ?"

"Not that I know of Has anyone heard of experiments being made on elephants' hearing ?"

Last Christmas I had read a detailed but fascinating study called The Physiology of the Elephant by Benedict. He gave all sorts of interesting figures connected with muscular activity, respiration rate, ventilation of lungs, total basal metabolism and even the amount of methane in the air from the trunk due to intestinal fermentation ! But nothing had I read about acoustics so could happily say: "I don't think so. There's an American named Benedict who's done a lot of work on elephants but he doesn't mention it."

"After that red herring," someone said jokingly, "I suggest that the shape of the back is the next most obvious difference. The African has a concave dip, like a horse, while Jumbo has a convex dome."

Therefore an Indian elephant is more useful !

And so the conversation went on in the lamplight with contributions for most people who had done their homework before the expedition !

A couple of days later a newly arrived reporter asked me a further question about elephants, while we walked along the dusty footpath.

"Could you tell me, sir, why you are taking an Indian elephant across the Alps when Hannibal took African ?" Ah, I had been waiting for this one, so asked Mr. X. "How do you know he took African ?" He shrugged his shoulders and said : " Well, he came from Africa so I suppose he took native elephants." Another member of the expedition had joined us and together we produced our arguments for the pressman.

"Firstly, our sources of information on the subjects are Carthaginian coins. A number of these have been found with a magnificent image of an elephant on one side." I took out my note-book and showed him a sketch I had made of a coin minted by the Carthaginians in Spain, only two years before Hannibal's crossing. It bore the clear indications of an African elephant and as the conversation of two nights before had brushed up my knowledge, there was no difficulty in pointing them out . . . the large ears, concave back, flat hindquarters, head held erect, flat forehead, and so on. The reporter nodded gleefully. So far he was obviously winning

126

his point and said: "The elephant which posed as model for this coin was probably one of the very ones which crossed with Hannibal." But then my team-mate broke in with, "Where's that sketch of the Etrurian coin, John ?" and when I had produced it he said triumphantly:

"Now this coin shows an Indian elephant. See the hump back, the small ear and profile of forehead ! It was minted in 2 1 7 B. c., the year after Hannibal had reached Italy and is Etrurian. On its other side, of which unfortunately we have no drawing, is the head of an African negro. Etruria lay on Hannibal's line of march and as there is no record of any other elephants being brought through the area could we not assume that Hannibal influenced its design and that he had Indian elephants as well as African !"

The reporter nodded in agreement. "But," he asked, "from where could Hannibal have got Indian elephants ?"

"The answer may sound surprising," I said, "but probably from Egypt. I am told that Pharaoh had captured a number in his Syrian campaigns and as Egypt and Carthage were strongly allied in the first Carthaginian war against Rome, there is little doubt that Indian elephants, from Syria, were sent along the north coast of Africa as part of the supplies from Pharaoh." My friend cut in ... "Cato recorded that the elephant which fought most valiantly in Hannibal's campaign was called 'Sums'. This means 'the Syrian' and is another proof that at least one of Hannibal's elephants was Indian."

The reporter looked really interested. We were delighted when he said he wanted to write about this for his paper. After all, one of our most important aims was to make the public turn with new interest to history. The study of coins can convey a wealth of information. Our reporter scribbled some notes in his own language and hurried off down the hillside to the waiting taxi on the main road. As I watched him go I wished that other pressmen would come up with such questions and be just as interested in an aspect of the journey that could easily be dwarfed in the excitement of Jumbo in action. One could hardly blame them, however, for she was such an intriguing animal !

The question of which type of elephant Hannibal had used leads us on to the next, which is: "Why did Hannibal bring elephants at alb"

I feel that the main reason lies in their effect on cavalry. In the world of that time cavalry was the most strategic arm of any army. It was fast moving and flexible. At the battle of Cannae it was the cavalry engagement that swayed the battle and led to the complete surrounding of the Roman forces. To produce a successful anti-cavalry weapon was no mean achievement and Hannibal had evident pride in the effect of his elephants. They frightened the horses with their enormous size, noise of trumpeting and, we are told, smell ! They were also trained to fight and one can imagine the terrifying effect of Hannibal's thirty-seven elephants all charging in line, lunging forward with their tusks and trampling down the enemy foot-soldiers with their forefeet. Elephants could also be used as look,-out points and self-propelled batteries of fire- power, for they were well able to carry towers (think of the Elephant and Castle) which provided a comfortable vantage point for sling-throwers and archers. Finally, Hannibal discovered that his elephants were extremely useful in the Alpine areas where the enemy tribes had never seen such strange beasts before. It seems that they must have regarded them with strong religious fear for Hannibal's army was never attacked in that section where the elephants were. Here surely are good enough arguments to show that Hannibal considered worth while the trouble of taking elephants. They were not always an asset to his following. On the steep and treacherous descent from the summit pass he came to such a difficult point that it took three days to make it passable for his elephants. Those were three crucial days, for his men starved and no doubt would have gladly eaten raw elephant meat.

Having seen that there was method in Hannibal's madness let us turn to our elephant, a descendant, in spirit if not in blood, of those historic pachyderm.

Jumbo, otherwise known as Hannibella, had been born in Bombay State, India, in the autumn of 1947. Arduino Terni, a well-known dealer in animals, bought her and, when she was ten months old, brought her by ship to Italy. Evidently she had not enjoyed the sea voyage and kept the sailors awake at night. Arduino found that the only way to keep her quiet was to stay up and provide her with a constant supply of milk. That winter she was sold to the famous Circus Togni and grew up in the sawdust atmosphere. That is why she can walk so cleverly on a row of eight-inch diameter posts, a foot off the ground, and is guaranteed as sure-footed on the narrowest of paths. Almost exactly ten years later, Arduino bought her back for his prize zoo at Turin and set to work training her for the Alpine crossing.

There were several interesting aspects of elephant life which we saw demonstrated by Jumbo. Colonel Hickman had already given me a very informative list of observations made from the experience of the British Army in India.

(1) Elephants can only move at a walk but for short distances may proceed at a fast shuffle up of to 15 m.p.h.

(2) Army elephants, under load, will march 15 to 20 miles a day. They average 5 to 6 hours per day at 3 m.p.h.

(3) They are more suitable as beasts of burden than for traction. Will pull a 4.5 howitzer only 5 miles a day with frequent stops.

(4) Mature elephants can be expected to carry a 1,200-lb. load. In the Abyssinian campaign they carried anything from 1,500 to 1,800 lb.

(5) They get footsore if worked for several days on wet or rocky ground or metalled roads. Boots will soon wear out unless fitted with an iron shoe.

(6) They are quite incapable of making the slightest leap. Therefore as the maximum stride is about 6 feet, a 7-ft. ditch is completely impassable.

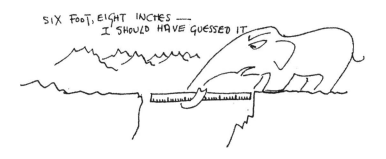

SIX FOOT, EIGHT INCHES —
I SHOULD HAVE GUESSED IT

(7) They have sensitive skins and cannot stand extremes of heat or cold. It is particularly dangerous if they are cold and wet, from rain or sleet, at the same time. They chill easily. (This was very important to note for our journey.)

(8) They dislike small animals, and especially dogs.

(9) In the army they were found to be unreliable in battle and did not stand firm against gunfire.

(It looks as if the Carthaginians had special techniques for training their elephants and controlling them in battle. The fact that they used the African species which today is considered totally unreliable when grown up, augments this.)

(10) Food requirements per day: Grain 15 lb.; Dry Fodder 200 lb. ; Salt 2 oz. and oil 1 oz. A third of the grain ration should be given first thing in the morning prior to work. At night there should be sufficient fodder to last until 1O p.m.

(11) They sleep for only 4 hours a night but often doze, and either lie down or stand up. (In strange surroundings Jumbo always stood up.)

(12) If they lie down facing downhill they are unable to get up. It is important that they are shackled facing uphill, on uneven ground. (I have often wondered how you get one of these poor benighted elephants on its feet again ! —perhaps a breakdown van can put a chain around its neck and lift.)

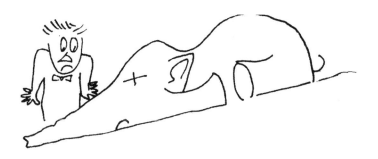

(13) They must be watered at least twice a day. On an average they drink 30 to 50 gallons a day. They should not be permitted to drink if hot but may be permitted to take small quantities on line of march, if continuing. (We found this exactly so, in the case of Jumbo.)

While on the subject of drinking, a veterinary friend had written to me: 'Drinking water might be a problem, since the higher you go, the colder the water, and this might affect the elephant adversely. You should have facilities, therefore, for taking the chill off water, several gallons of which will be drunk.' When it came to the test, we were able to rely completely on Jumbo as to whether water was too cold for her or not. She did not even have to put her trunk into it to tell. The sensitive tip could, no doubt, discern the temperature just above its surface. Fortunately we never had to use heating equipment at high altitude but one can just imagine the kind of apparatus Heath Robinson would have visualised!

Jumbo with the team

Expedition assembles for the start

Send-off from Montmélian

A welcome cool-off—at Aiguebelle

Fitting Jumbo's boots and jacket

Trying on her boot

Campfire, Jumbo and small guitar

Camp life with an elephant

Jumbo drinks from an Alpine river—near the 'bare rock'

The night march

Jumbo negotiates a narrow bridge

Up and over

Under Caesar's Triumphal Arch, Susa

Dancers surround Jumbo at Susa

138

Victory cake in Italy

Dealing with some of the other points on the Colonel's list:

It was quite easy to tell whether Jumbo was overheated or too cold. One did not need an elephant-size thermometer, though, no doubt, that is what Benedict had to use before he could produce the fact that the temperature of the air expired from the tip of the trunk is 31°C. All Ernesto did was to feel under the elephant's arm pit and this method proved a very good indication. We all learnt to do it and were taught exactly what rectifying action was needed for each condition.

Point two indicates the reasonable distance a normal elephant will cover in a day. Although ours was not loaded, nor do we believe that Hannibal's were as they proved too valuable as weapons of war to be used as baggage animals, the figures coincide well with the daily marching distances of an army in the condition of Hannibal's.

I have always been intrigued by the inability of the elephant to jump, and if one remembers also its fear of dogs, one would imagine that in olden days an almost impregnable defence against elephant attack would be a seven-foot trench and a pack of dogs. If elephants were the tanks of the ancient world, a pack of dogs, specially trained to attack them in the rear, would have been excellent anti-tank weapons !

Most Alpine villages would have their normal collection of dogs and Jumbo hated these with a hatred born of experience. An important job for the team was to chase off any of these inquisitive creatures which might be too near. While our party was really high up, we had to be careful not to camp in an area where there might be marmots. These squirrel-like animals live at high altitude, in holes in the rock, and once again because they are small, can genuinely alarm any elephant. We have never seen Jumbo with a mouse but imagine that she would be even more terrified. After all, it might run up her trunk or one of her legs. ·

Apart from this strong dislike for small, fast-moving things, what did we see of Jumbo's character and intelligence? After all, you may say, with such a huge brain she must certainly have some thinking power ! I went into the matter and sadly have to report that intelligence is not proportional to brain size or to its weight. It is the ratio of weight of brain to total weight of body which matters and this is where Jumbo and her kind come unstuck. Although her brain weighs nearly four times as much as ours she is forty times as heavy!

140

Nevertheless, elephants are well known for their intelligence and Jumbo was no exception to the rule.

I think her sense of humour and fun were what struck us most. It was not only that she had a perpetual smile on her face but that this expression would change in a subtle way according to conditions. She thoroughly enjoyed the happy atmosphere of the journey and periodically showed this by flapping her ears and waving her trunk. It was not often that she would express her feelings vocally but she made delighted little grunts whenever Arduino came up to speak to her. Going to the other extreme, only once did we hear her bloodcurdling scream of rage and fear trumpeting through the mountains. We blame the gods of the tempest. Her complete enjoyment of making people happy must have come from circus days and she could sense this holiday atmosphere when blowing the harmonica. Her pleasure at being spoken to was very evident and brought a response if not in kind then in spirit.

She developed strong likes and dislikes for people and by the end of the expedition had made up her mind about every member of the team and a good number of the Press. I always thought it most interesting that she practically fell in love with Jimmy, her only companion from the East. They were the greatest of pals.

Her patience and stamina were very evident during the crises in the journey. The night march did not put her off her stride in the slightest and she was always most obliging and willing to fall in with the plans of the rest of us ! Of course most of this good behaviour was almost certainly due to Ernesto's careful control and the common bond of understanding which the two had. However, she was not always an angel! There were moments when she had made up her mind to do something and do it she would-no matter what Ernesto, or the team, or the crowds, or the Press, or the whole world thought.

The proverbial saying goes 'Elephants never forget'. Jumbo's memory seemed pretty good, particularly when it came to food and where it was kept, and she would recognise certain people in an instant. That she will always remember her journey over the Alps goes without question. Whether she will be able to recall the varied personalities that surrounded her is not quite so certain. She hinted that she would do her best!

We leave her, as we left her at the end of the last chapter, quietly munching her supper back at home with the members of the expedition whispering sweet nothings into her big ear and asking her not to forget them.

CHAPTER XIX

Roman Holiday

WE WERE GOING to Rome. This would m itself have been
enough cause for happy expectation. But we were being invited there
by the 'Organismo Rappresentative Universitario Romano'. This is
the huge Association to which every student at Rome belongs.
Guiseppe Sicari, a medical student, had given himself unstintingly to
arranging a reception and had been appointed 'President of the Rome
Reception Committee for the British Alpine Hannibal Expedition'.
We were impressed not only by this title but also by his organising
ability. If Rome received Hannibal's army with hatred and fear, the
new Carthaginians were to see what exactly was meant by the lavish
hospitality of Romans. Only four of us could go as the others had to
hurry back to England but our party, consisting of Ernesto, Cynthia,
Richard and myself was now joined by Laura, Ernesto's fiancee. We
left Turin in the expedition car, two days after our arrival there with
Jumbo. The first night was spent in Florence where a catastrophe
against which we had been warned occurred. The car was broken
into and a suitcase stolen. Next morning when the awful discovery
had been made, we paled at the thought of being kept waiting all day
long at police stations while a reception committee, grown to an
enormous size in our vivid imaginations, waited agitatedly at Rome.
Forces would have to split. The infantry stayed to give peace tokens
to the Florentine police while the cavalry rode on at the pace of Jehu,
to Rome itself This strategy proved successful for not only was
Rome taken (by surprise to see us there almost on time) but also the
case and its contents were found, most mysteriously, and handed
over by the police. We could hardly believe our good fortune. Either
the Florentine thieves are different from all other thieves the world
over or the police there are wizards.

I looked at the programme proposed for the next few days and felt
rather overwhelmed. It seemed incredible that so much had been
planned for our entertainment but here stood the indefatigable
Giuseppe P.R.R.C.F.T.B.A.H.E. right in front of me nodding
agreeably. There were to be concerts, operas, visits to museums, the
Imperial forum, excavations, and the Shelley and Keats memorials.
We were to be presented to the Lord Mayor of Rome at the

143

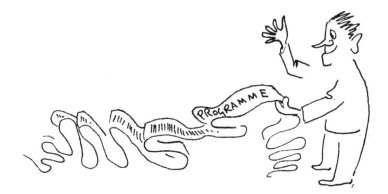

Capital and to attend a special ceremony at the University (though we did not know what this was for) and finally there was the main purpose of our visit, a lecture on the expedition in the Salla Borromini, by kind permission of the Lord Mayor. Now the Salla Borromini was the most splendid setting in Rome for 'intimate' lectures and elegantly printed invitations had been sent to a large number of the intelligentsia of the city. As I walked up the centre aisle of the resplendent baroque hall, at our dress rehearsal, and gazed up at its painted ceiling, I realised the glory of our position and its demands on us. We had grappled with an academic problem and made a practical test to try to prove our theory, and now we were brought to the very capital of the country most concerned with that problem, placed in the finest and grandest lecture hall available and invited to explain our findings. It all made such excellent sense, was so proper, so right, such a superb and appropriate ending to the whole expedition. I could not have been more delighted. If we were able to meet this challenge and make out a case before the professors and intellectuals of Rome we would be able to do so anywhere.

But before the night of the lecture the university seemed to have given us a programme so delightful as to entice even the weariest of travellers but so strenuous as to make us suspect that our hosts planned to tire us out before ever the Borromini ordeal took place. We were already almost exhausted. The strain of the Alpine journey and long motor ride, added to by robbery, was beginning to tell and our siestas were long and deep. Most of the visits had to be cut out. However, in the cool of the evenings we were ushered out of the hotel and enjoyed the beautiful floodlit fountains of Frascati, an indescribably impressive performance of' Aida' at the Terme di Caracalla, a Mozart-Pizzetti concert at the open-air Domitian Stadium and other delights.

The 'Hannibal idea' seemed to have caught on, for on the very day that the expedition had set out from Montmelian Warner Brothers of America and Liber Film of Italy began to shoot their film, 'Hannibal', right here in Rome. Victor Mature and Rita Gamm were taking the leading roles. Naturally, we were eager to see what was happening so we took our car, together with two members of the reception committee, and drove off to the woods beyond the city. The first signs of the unusual was a Carthaginian soldier, in full armour, sitting by the roadside lighting a twentieth-century cigarette. He directed us on and eventually we came to the Carthaginian camp set in a lovely birch-wood. Soldiers were sitting about talking. The odd chariot, spears and catapults, littered the ground. All that could be seen of Victor Mature was a pair of very muscular legs poised horizontally in mid air, beyond the half-opened door of a shack. He was resting. We chatted to Rita Gamm while waiting for something interesting to happen.

Suddenly there was a lot of shouting and a herd of young elephants stampeded through the camp. We stood spell-bound. I was amazed that no one was hurt but evidently the whole thing had been well under control. In a few minutes, when the odd tent had been propped up again, the scene was repeated. By this time 'Hannibal' himself (Victor Mature) had joined us and before long we were deep

145

in discussion. I was keen to know all about the film. Where was the crossing of the Alps to be filmed ? What kind of man was Hannibal to be ? Did they bring out the fact that the elephants were most useful against cavalry ? I had a whole host of questions to ask. But our party had to leave about half-way through the afternoon to prepare for the mysterious reception at the university. Much as we looked forward to this, it was with reluctant feet that we left the silver birch-wood, our only glimpse of Carthaginian camp life as Hannibal might have seen it. Picture that scene at La Praz or L'Esseillon, high in the Alps, and you might well see a section of Hannibal's army as it must have looked in the autumn of 218 B.C.

We arrived at the university by car-but it had nearly been by chariot ! The plan was to borrow one of the magnificent chariots used for the film, hire a charioteer and race up to the university at full gallop. Chariot, driver and horse were available. The only reason why the plan never materialised was that the police would not allow

it. I suppose there were no regulations in the Italian highway code for chariots so, rather than let the policeman on point duty get himself into an awkward situation by giving preference to a chariot while the other drivers hooted indignantly, they took the safer line.

We were shown up to a large first-floor hall, introduced to a wide variety of people, students, members of the staff and a large party of English teachers, in Rome on an exchange scheme. We were not at first over-delighted to meet so large a party of our compatriots, who, we suspected, might regard our joyous plan to arrive by chariot with somewhat jaundiced eyes. However, it was not long before we discovered that they were all as gay and delightful as the Romans. We began to sense that proceedings were not to be altogether serious.

The ceremony itself was conducted entirely by students, senior members of O.R.U.R., who entered dressed in their long, scarlet

146

robes of office and extraordinary hats with nine-inch, pointed peaks. There was an immediate hush as two solemn figures proceeded to the centre of the room, chanting strange and, no doubt, magical phrases in Latin.

We stood in a row before the table and tried to look intelligent. After a long Latin speech each of us stepped forward in turn and was invested with a gaily-coloured peaked hat and then heartily embraced; embraced twice, I may say, with head first on one and then the other of the opposite's shoulders. As each wore the nine-inch peaked cap, a vigorous sway-back motion in between embraces was the only way to prevent collision of hats and general disorder. All this was regarded with great hilarity by the spectators. Medals were presented and the climax came when Guiseppe himself presented us with a magnificent Latin scroll, beautifully engrossed on parchment, commemorating the visit and paying due homage to Hannibal and Jumbo. Apart from an elephant boot it is my most prized souvenir.

The civic presentation next day was a more serious affair. Our car swept up the steep winding drive to the Capitol and there in the piazza designed by Michelangelo stood Guiseppe, as punctual as ever, immaculately dressed and waiting to lead us in. A dream had become reality. Here we were entering the holy of holies of Roman government-the Capitol itself If Hannibal had captured the city it was from this very spot that he would have promulgated the new laws for Carthaginianising Rome and introduced the worship of Baal, replacing that of Jupiter, Juno and Minerva. The sacred geese of Juno, descendents of those which, by their apprehensive cackling, had saved the Capitol from surprise Gallic attacks 173 years earlier, would have been destroyed. He must have dreamt of this spot during the long cold nights in the Alps. This is where his heart had been fixed ever since his early vow in the temple.

We were led through a maze of ante-rooms into a large chamber beautifully decorated with tapestries and made to sit at a long table on velvet-covered armchairs. We were told in a reverent whisper that the Mayor had been unable to come but the Deputy Mayor would receive us instead. Members of the university, government officials and pressmen crowded in and we all rose as the small figure of the Deputy Mayor appeared through large double doors at the end of the room. The ceremony was simple. Mayors and Deputy Mayors are well known for their verbosity. This gentleman was no exception but he was also a born orator ! The words rolled out in a torrent of eloquence. Spoken Italian is delightful to the ear even when but little understood. Now we were able to lean back and enjoy it to the full. A few words, such as Annibale and La spedizione di Jumbo could be recognised but the main points of the oration could only be guessed. For the speaker this was an 'historic occasion'. It certainly was for the team! Having been presented with a beautifully illustrated book on Rome, we replied with a shorter and, inevitably, less eloquent speech of thanks and presented an ornate album of expedition photographs, which traced its progress from Montmelian to Turin.

The great day for the lecture in the Salla Borromini had come. Richard and I spent the afternoon going through coloured slides and discussing presentation technique and then carefully groomed ourselves for the occasion. Cynthia was waiting for us in the hotel foyer and we stepped out into the cool evening air. Ernesto and Laura would come later. They were involved in some last-minute shopping. The Salla Borromini looked lovelier still in the soft lamplight and after a pause to absorb the atmosphere we set to work to put everything in order; gave slides into the hands of the projectionist and placed a programme on every seat. These programmes had been beautifully produced for us in Turin and were profusely illustrated. They bore two blocks of Italian writing. One briefly described Hannibal's journey: the other explained the technique of investigation used by the expedition and told something of the journey. To have a programme like this was at least a moral boost for, as Richard said to me while we waited behind stage, even if we broke down or were reduced to continuous stuttering under the strain of the occasion, the learned of Rome could still carry away a clear statement of the facts.

However, all went well. We strode on to the stage, one each side of our charming young lady interpreter. She was there to try and make us intelligible to the Italians. Richard spoke first and he led off with a brief description of the Carthaginian wars and dwelt in detail on Hannibal's Alpine crossing. He invited everyone to turn to their programme where, on a rough map of the Mediterranean basin, a dotted line indicated Hannibal's route. Speeding on through the old, old story, he dwelt for a few minutes on Hannibal's character. This was the best part of his speech, and fortunately our interpreter did a wonderful job in translating him.

I then took his place and began my explanation of' How to take an elephant over the Alps'. Acting on the principle that visual aids provide the most effective method of teaching, I showed a large number of slides. These were very successful, as pictures of an elephant surrounded by mountains are bound to be, and our interpreter struggled valiantly against the difficulties of rendering my words into Italian. How could she attempt to translate " ... and so Jumbo forged a trunk route over the Alps" and still retain the play upon words. However, she was obviously delighted at the ease of rendering my final sentence, that about the peaceful, inter-continental Hanniballistic elephant. After all, the word ballistic has the same meaning in Italian and English.

I was relieved at the kindness with which the audience received our lecture. After all, their ancestors had cried "Hannibal ad portas", when ours were mere barbarians. On the face of it, it was temerarious to come to the heart of Hannibal country and raise our voices.

The lights were switched on and the audience sat up with a start when, having donned our peaked caps, Richard and I presented the University with a large parcel; an unorthodox but calculated action. After much strenuous unpacking the contents were re- revealed. It was an elephant boot and the literati of Rome, instead of coming up and saying " What you have been saying is complete nonsense", lost themselves in the complexities of elephant-boot design. Whether or not they wanted to call the theory utter nonsense we shall never know. All we knew was that we had stated our case clearly and that Jumbo's boot had come into its own. Hannibal was not the only strategist to provide a diversionary ruse !

Next morning, at 5.0 a.m. the expedition car set off for the distant island of Britain. Behind us was a boot and, we hoped, an increased number of Hanniphils.

CHAPTER XX

Reflections

THE TEAM SCATTERED. Richard took the car back to England, Cynthia went to her family in Germany, Ernesto and Laura remained in Turin and I was alone at the foot of the Alps, with seven glorious days in which to do exactly as I liked. There seemed no reason why I should want to climb up to the passes of Mont Cenis and Clapier again. If it was a matter of having time on my hands why didn't I go to the Dolomites, for they had always fascinated me and demanded exploration? The Italian Lakes or Venice or a hundred and one other places would be equally worth a visit, nevertheless it was to Mont Cenis and Clapier that I went; they drew me as a magnet.

One morning I set off from Susa, well shod and with rucksack, sleeping-bag, sketchbook and camera. A motor-cyclist took me part of the way and after a stiff climb I reached my first goal, the high plateau of the Grand Mont Cenis pass. I sat down beside the lake, had my sandwich lunch, sketched and took some photo- graphs. The austere and beautiful landscape had laid a new and solemn spell upon me. I felt that I was looking at it through different eyes, for the experience of the last three weeks had changed us all. The solitude and quiet were soothing. How precious these were after the excitement and responsibility of the expedition journey. My aim was to spend the night on the Col de Clapier, all alone and, no doubt, with the ghost of Hannibal to haunt me, but now lingered on the Mont Cenis pass for a while. I loved this pass, and, besides, Hannibal had probably sent at least some of his men over it.

By cutting across country to the Petit Mont Cenis Pass, above La Crosta, and turning sharp left, one can reach Clapier from the west. A steady, gentle climb of several hours brought me at last to the small lake just below its summit. It was getting late and the evening sun appeared to rest on the jagged buttresses of the Dent d' Ambin. I walked the last few hundred yards, unstrapped the rucksack and threw myself on the ground. On one side, in the ever lengthening shadows, the mountain buttresses plunged down into

Italy; on the other, the lake shone like silver beneath the setting sun; and beyond, in stately dignity, lay the misty blue and purple giants of the French Alps. This was the moment for which I had been waiting. I sat and gazed, with a new sense of reverence.

Memories of the last three weeks came flooding into my mind, the rollicking hilarity and silent joy, moments of difficulty, and others of success. I opened my wallet and pulled out a small piece of paper. On it were typed the aims of the expedition. It had accompanied us throughout the journey and now, once more, I read it through.

1. *To prove that Hannibal had used the Clapier route*

You may remember the short appendix to Thor Heyerdahl's world famous book The Kon-Tiki Expedition. He wrote modestly; 'My migration theory as such was not proved by the successful outcome of the Kon-Tiki expedition' (i.e. the journey of a balsa raft from Peru to the Pacific Islands). What it had proved, he claimed, was that the balsa raft possessed qualities hitherto unsuspected by modern scientists, and that the Pacific Islands were well within reach of Peru, even with prehistoric craft. With such an example before me I cannot put too high the claims of my own expedition. As Heyerdahl had learnt something new about pre- historic craft, we, in our turn, had learnt something new about elephants. If an elephant is young and fit, it need not be affected by altitude.

This has not been the result gained by previous recorded experiments in taking elephants to high altitudes. Richard Halliburton's elephant had been only a few years older than Jumbo, yet it had suffered severely from scarcity of oxygen at 6,500 feet above sea- level. 'Elephant Bill' took a herd over the Chin hills from Burma to Assam during the war, and he records that when they passed the 5,000-foot line the animals, especially the older ones, were pain- fully slow at climbing. Admittedly, Jumbo was in perfect physical condition, and she had been given strenuous exercise before she made her climb, but that does not detract from the successful findings of the expedition.

By showing that an elephant could climb to over 7,000 feet without undue difficulty, we demonstrated that the distances between the strategic points on the Isere-Arc-Clapier route could have been covered by an elephant within the time-table laid down by Polybius. This does not, however, prove conclusively that Hannibal did use this route. He merely could have done. There is still room for arguments in favour of other passes, and I have no doubt that there will be plenty of argument.

From our observations on altitude, and the records kept of speed, distance and time, it can be argued that Hannibal's nine- day march to the summit pass fits with the conditions between Pontcharra and the Col de Clapier, and above all, that the distance between the 'bare rock' at L'Esseillon and the Col de Clapier could have been covered comfortably by an elephant in a night and a day. We had contributed the idea of a night march, but apart from this we had no radically new conclusions. This new knowledge added a little more weight to the Clapier theory, and removed one of the most important objections to it, but it did not constitute proof, it was only a demonstration of possibility. I might even add that our decision not to take Jumbo up the last few miles was in accord with Hannibal's difficulties in passing over it. We had proved that the relative speeds and distances covered on this route could have been those described by Polybius.

2. To make a complete photographic record of the expedition

This had been accomplished and every aspect covered: the strategic points, the road surfaces, slope of the paths and views of the way ahead as Hannibal would have seen them. This record is too detailed to be published in a book of this size and nature. However, it has been fully entered in the expedition log-book which will be available for future investigators.

3. Archeological Survey

Although possible tumuli had been sighted on the Col de Clapier they had not been promising enough to warrant investigation. This line of approach has been left for future and expert archeologists. It

152

is certain that unless Carthaginian relics are found in the Alps in some quantity the riddle of Hannibal's route will never be completely solved.

4. *Popularisation of History*

This aim had been achieved beyond our wildest hopes. It was very agreeable to discover articles in British, French and Italian papers which used the expedition to explain the fascination of the problem and the relevance of ancient history. People were not just entertained by the idea of an elephant walking over the Alps. History to them had become alive.

5. *To promote International Friendship*

This aim was also achieved beyond our hopes. The members of the team had certainly gained a fresh understanding of the French and Italians. They no doubt saw a new facet of British life and enthusiasm. En route, one old French lady went up to Colonel Hickman and asked what all the commotion was about. He laughingly replied: "A great big beast an elephant-is coming up the valley."

She asked: "Who is bringing it?" "The British."

"That explains it !" she remarked.

The many friendships which have been made as a result of the expedition will not be easily broken.

6. *To make a contribution for World Refugee Year*

It was still uncertain how much money there would be, once all the expenses had been covered, but our final aim of providing £750 for the World Refugee Year was by no means beyond possibility. We had decided that the money should not be lost in the great central fund but given to one particular needy cause. The Ockenden Venture provides a very lovely home in England for refugee children of Europe in particular need. The money would be donated to this worthy cause, to assist a boy or a girl of the Venture's choosing. £750 is the cost of five years' living and schooling in England.

7. The last aim on my piece of paper was to meet the demand for self discipline, careful thinking and wise action. We did our best, we went all out for the one great aim. We made some mistakes but we learnt more than we can say.

It was getting dark. I folded my piece of paper and stuffed it away but thought of the many other lessons we learnt.

Firstly, as regards the elephant, we learnt something of its physiology, habits and reactions to changing conditions.

Secondly, concerning Hannibal's descent from the Col de Clapier. In 1956 we thought Hannibal descended straight down from the pass to the Claree river. Through the expedition, we met Dr. M. A. de Lavis-Trafford who pointed out how Polybius' conditions fit in far more satisfactorily if Hannibal descended by the Savine Coche exit from Clapier and then followed a horizontal though difficult path over to the south, leading to Les Quatre Dents ridge and Chaumont. Having studied the two routes on the spot, I agree with him.

Thirdly, were it not for the expedition we would never have heard of Major Alixant's theory, which appeared in the paper, Dauphine Libere, half-way through the journey. He fully agreed with us and mentioned strange markings on the side of the ascent to Clapier which, he believes, were made by the Carthaginians.

Finally, we would never have heard of Senator Sibille's theory of Hannibal using three passes simultaneously. An interesting project would be to send an elephant over each and note their relative speeds.

These were the matters over which I pondered as the sun went down beyond the Vanois Glacier and as I sat on the very ground Hannibal probably used to harangue his men two thousand years

154

ago. I switched on my torch, hoisted the rucksack and clambered down to where a ruined hut, of which I knew, would give shelter for the night.

Chronological Diary of the Expedition

A. *The deed and its aftermath*

October 218 B.C.   Hannibal crosses Alps.

216 B.C.   Battle of Cannae.

203 B.C.   Hannibal leaves Italy.

183 B.C.   Hannibal commits suicide.

B. *The first two witnesses*

151 B.C.   Polybius crosses Alps in Hannibal's footsteps
and later writes on it.

20 B.C.   Livy writes on crossing.

C. *Others express their views*

The following are some of those who support the Isere-Arc-
Mont Cenis and or Clapier theory :

1574   Josias Sirrler.

1816   Napoleon.

1826   J. L. Laranza.

1835   R. Ellis.

1887   Colonel Perrin.

1898   W. H. Bullock Hall.

1900   W. Osiander.

1902   P. Azan.

1904   J. Colin.

1911   Spencer Wilkinson.

1925   H. Ferrand.

1956   Dr. A. H. McDonald.

1956   Dr. M.A. de Lavis-Trafford.

1958   Professor Walbank.

1959   Major Alixant.

D. *Looking at the ground*

1956 *The Alps*

June 3rd   Cambridge Hannibal Expedition formed.

Aug 15th   Expedition leaves England.

Aug 24th   Assault on Col. de Clapier.

Aug 25th   Assault on Col. de Mont Genevre.

Aug 27th   Assault on Col. de la Traversette.

Sept 8th   Return to England.

1957 *The Pyrenees*

July-August   A two-member team studies crossing by Le
    Perthus pass.

E. A practical test   The time-distance study

1958   Nov. 18th   Initial idea conceived.

Dec. 13th   Elephant made available by Turin Zoo.

1959   June 8th   Team complete.

June 13th   Team Conference at Cambridge.

June 14th   Elephant jacket completed.

July 3rd   Contract with Life Magazine finalised.

July 9th   Contract with News Chronicle finalised.

July 12th   Elephant boots completed.

July 13th   Full insurance agreement completed.

July 14th   Final Team conference with Dr. McDonald at
     Cambridge.

July 17th   Ernesto and Jumbo leave Turin for starting
point by train. Richard and Michael leave England by car
with equipment.

July 18th   Colonel Hickman, Clare, Cynthia, Jimmy and
John leave England by train ferry.

July 19th   Expedition assembles at starting point. Fete.

July 20th   Start. March: Montmelian to La Rochette via
     Pontcharra (Ascent towards the Alps).

July 21st   March: La Rochette (' enemy town') to
Aiguebelle.

158

July 22nd	March: Aiguebelle to La Chambre.
July 23rd	March: La Chambre to St. Michel.
July 24th	March: St. Michel to La Praz.
July 25th	March: La Praz to L'Esseillon.
July 26th	March: L'Esseillon to Le Planey (night journey).
July 27th	March: Le Planey to Termignon.
July 28th	March: Termignon to Col du Grand Mont Cenis.
July 29th	Descent to Italy-Col to Susa.
July 31st	Grand entry into Turin.
Aug 1st	1st Colonel Hickman, Clare, Michael and Jimmy return to England by train.
Aug 2nd	The others leave Turin for Rome by car.
Aug 7th	FINALE : Lecture in Salla Borromini, Rome.

APPENDIX II

A comparison of the Passes claimed as Hannibal's

(for those who want an interesting, energetic holiday in the Alps)

Instructions: Study the conditions as stated by Polybius, walk over the nine contestant passes and see if the conditions fit the terrain. If you agree with me that the Col de Clapier has the strongest claim, with runners-up in the two Mount Cenis passes, do write and let me know. I shall be delighted. For that matter, write, whatever your conclusions. Any new light will be valuable.

The Conditions

Hannibal's pass must—

(a) be large enough to camp 30,000 men and about 5,000 horses (on its French side)

(b) command a panoramic view of the Po valley

(c) have a difficult descent

(d) be high enough to have large areas of snow, from two consecutive winters on its flanks

(e) have a place for pasturing the horses immediately after the difficult stretch of the descent

(f) give a distance of three days' march, from here to the plains.

(g) lead straight down to the land of the Turini.

160

(h) be a day's march from a probable site for the 'bare-rock' ambush (or a day and a night for the baggage and elephants).

(i) be positioned so that the most direct route to it from the Rhone passes by the 'Island' (where the river 'Skaras' meets the Rhone) seven days' march from the sea (three days from the sea to the crossing of the Rhone and four from the crossing to the Island).

The following table gives purely my personal opinion as to the fitting of the conditions to the passes. Five marks are awarded to a complete fit and less for more doubtful cases.

Northern	Altitude (ft.a.s.l.)	a	b	c	d	e	f	g	h	i	Total
Little St. Bernard Pass	7,179	2	0	3	3	2	0	0	5	5	20
Central (from Isère-Arc River)											
Col du Grand Mont Cenis	6,893	3	0	4	2	5	3	5	3	5	30
Col du Petit Mont Cenis	7,150	3	0	4	3	5	3	5	5	5	33
Col de Clapier	8,173	5	5	5	4	5	3	5	5	5	42
South (from Durance River)											
Col de Mont Genèvre	6,083	5	0	3	2	3	5	5	5	1	29
Col de l'Echelle	5,900	5	0	5	1	5	5	5	0	1	27
Col de Bousson	7,014	5	0	0	3	2	5	5	5	1	26
Col de la Traversette	9,760	0	5	5	5	3	5	0	2	1	26
Col de Larche (Argentière)	6,600	5	0	2	2	3	5	0	3	1	21

Manufactured by Amazon.ca
Bolton, ON

34436871R00094